ON EARTH AS IT IS IN HEAVEN

ON EARTH AS IT IS IN HEAVEN

A FAITH-BASED TOOLKIT FOR ECONOMIC JUSTICE

ERIC ATCHESON

CHURCH
PUBLISHING
INCORPORATED

Church Publishing
19 East 34th Street
New York, NY 10016
www.churchpublishing.org

Cover design by Paul Soupiset
Typeset by Denise Hoff

Library of Congress Cataloging-in-Publication Data

Names: Atcheson, Eric, author.
Title: On earth as it is in heaven : a faith-based toolkit for economic
   justice / Eric Atcheson.
Identifiers: LCCN 2019048951 (print) | LCCN 2019048952 (ebook) | ISBN
   9781640652262 (paperback) | ISBN 9781640652279 (epub)
Subjects: LCSH: Economics--Religious aspects--Christianity. | Social
   justice--Religious aspects--Christianity.
Classification: LCC BR115.E3 A83 2020 (print) | LCC BR115.E3 (ebook) |
   DDC 261.8/5--dc23

LC record available at https://lccn.loc.gov/2019048951
LC ebook record available at https://lccn.loc.gov/2019048952

For Carrie, who is my love in every possible
and impossible sense.

For Sadie, who is my hope made flesh.
The love of generations is always at your back, my child.

And always, as my Jesuit alma mater would say,
for the greater glory of God. *Ad maiorem Dei gloriam.*

CONTENTS

PREFACE

For More than Ashes

My committee had just read over the first full draft of my doctoral thesis, and one of the members was intensely curious. Why did I title my project "For More than Ashes?"

I pointed toward the verse in Jeremiah where the prophet says that God has proclaimed, "People labor in vain; nations toil for nothing but ashes" (51:58).

He responded, "You need to make clear that verse's importance to you."

So, I did. You are holding the fruits of that years-long effort right now.

This book is inspired by my work as a doctor of ministry student at Seattle University's School of Theology and Ministry, where I wrote my thesis on a pair of labor union strikes that took place almost simultaneously in the late summer of 2015 in southwestern Washington State. At the time, I was pastoring a historic Disciples of Christ congregation in the area. Across Washington, public schoolteachers were going on strike in protest of the drastic privations imposed on them by a state legislature so dysfunctional that the state supreme court had held it in contempt for not approving a budget that passed constitutional muster the year prior.[1] Locally, the teachers who worked for the Kelso School District and were members of the Kelso Education Association labor union were among those who went on strike during those waves of protest.

Meanwhile, the millworkers at the pulp and paper mill owned by KapStone in Longview, across the Coweeman River from Kelso, had

---

1. Austin Jenkins, "Washington Supreme Court Finds State in Contempt," NW News Network, http://nwnewsnetwork.org/post/washington-supreme-court-finds-state-contempt, September 11, 2014, accessed July 23, 2018.

been laboring without a collective bargaining agreement for months, despite a series of protracted, on-and-off negotiations between Kap-Stone and the Association of Western Pulp and Paper Workers Local 153. After working without a contract since May 2014,[2] the members of AWPPW Local 153 went out on strike in 2015. It was the first time that Local 153 had done so in over thirty-five years, and they remained on strike for twelve days.

The close geographic and chronological proximity of both strikes shook the community in and around my former parish. I had congregants whose households were picketing and living on strike pay, and others (myself included) who attended rallies in solidarity with the teachers and millworkers. All around town, signs of support for the striking workers went up in the windows of homes and local businesses.

Beneath the outward signs of support, however, rumbled a genuine backlash toward the teachers, millworkers, and those who supported them. Furious letters were written to the editor of the local paper, *The Daily News*, denouncing the strikes. I began to receive unsigned hate mail at my church office. The striking workers still felt fear, stress, and trepidation as they took the leap of faith and courage to go on strike.

I know that because they told me so. In the autumn of 2017, just over two years after the strikes, I spent two months surveying union members who were also active in local congregations about their memories and feelings of the strikes and what they felt the church and the clergy could or should be doing to support them and help spiritually prepare them for the hardship of organizing and striking. I also surveyed those workers' pastors to also ask them about their own memories of the strikes and their beliefs about how the church should respond.

What the union members had to say surprised and inspired me. Their memories of the strikes were vivid and heartfelt, as they spoke

---

2. Marissa Luck, "Labor Board Says KapStone and Union Have Reached Impasse," *The Daily News*, https://tdn.com/news/local/labor-board-says-kapstone-and-union-have-reached-impasse/article_c6a3f52c-0e60-5661-b7ee-a5835db586a8.html, February 6, 2016, accessed July 23, 2018.

lovingly of the support they received as well as forthrightly about the worries they felt. Most—though not all—of them felt that the church had some role to play in the community during a strike. Even though they did not agree on what that role should look like, they did largely agree that they did not want the church, or their pastors, to simply pretend the strikes were not happening and that it was business as usual in their parishes. Most of all, the workers and pastors I polled expressed a necessity for the church to spiritually equip its congregants to encourage truth-telling, engagement, and dialogue over matters of labor and Christian spirituality the next time a labor action took place in their community.

That expressed need is what this book represents my attempt to meet: a need to equip laypeople and clergy alike with tools for truth-telling, fostering dialogue, and encouraging engagement with Christian social teaching about work. An integral part of this toolkit is an exploration of all of the benefits that it should confer: dignity, financial security, and a sense of pride in the fruits of one's own labors.

I have come by the desire and gumption to write this book the long way around. I spent nearly seven years embedded as a pastor in a community that had long relied on labor unions to protect the economic interests of its citizens, only for the unions to be decimated over decades of corporate indifference to the plights of poverty and financial insecurity in the area. Before my tenure as the pastor of First Christian Church in Longview, I lived and studied in the San Francisco Bay Area, which was rocked by the threat of a Bay Area Rapid Transit (BART) workers' strike in the summer of 2009. And as a boy, I was raised on the lessons of the gains organized workers had made for society by a father who worked as a lawyer for a firm that served Kansas City area labor unions before eventually being appointed as a state appellate judge.

I hope and pray that the passion of a life surrounded by the need for the poor and the workers to labor together for a better world shines through in these pages. I have come to believe that this sort of passion is what is required of the church—and, more broadly, of justice-minded people across the religious spectrum—to meaningfully change the economy we have constructed for ourselves over the past forty-some years in which the wealthy get wealthier while the rest of humanity simply survives—or does not survive.

More than any other experience, witnessing this macrocosmic trend play out on a more microcosmic level over the course of my first decade of parish ministry is what drove me toward God's lament in Jeremiah 51 of nations toiling for nothing but ashes. I have seen neighbors, siblings in Christ, and congregants turn themselves inside out both for their employers and for more than the crumbs from the table that their employers offered them. I have watched them try to sustain themselves on a diet of ashes, in a home built from ashes, on a salary of little more than ashes.

In the Bible, and during the Christian holiday of Ash Wednesday, ashes are a sign of repentance and humility. In gardening, ash can be a vital component of compost and fertilizer. But as a staple of a human diet, ashes have never been, and will never be, what physically sustains us. More is needed to nourish our God-created bodies. As much as other members of my faith may try to divorce the two for the sake of their own worldviews, Christianity and economics must engage each other when the economy is one that oppresses humanity in exchange for payouts of ashes.

This moral imperative has always existed throughout the church's history, even as both the church and the economic systems in question have changed dramatically over the course of that history. Understanding our role in that history is a necessary component to creating a better story going forward, and this book represents one tool with which to go about fulfilling that mandate. Integral to that task is an examination of the God-given mandates to pursue economic justice in both the Tanakh (Old Testament or Hebrew Bible) and the New Testament. This examination will cover how the texts might have been understood in their original contexts, interpreted throughout the history of the church, and, finally, imagined as a theological response to today's twenty-first-century capitalist economy.

This admittedly lofty aim intersects with a few other critical interests, including labor organizing and community activism, and one component of every chapter will be a discussion of potential action steps for pastors and laypeople to consider taking in their own communities. While I write from the vantage point and life experience of a pastor, this book was never designed to be exclusively for the clergy. In the true congregationalist spirit of my Disciples of Christ heritage, I hope that laypeople will co-lead alongside their pastors in this era-defining struggle for the Gospel's rightful place at the table of economic justice. This is not a clergy issue, and this is not a lay issue. This is a fundamentally human issue for which the Gospel of Jesus Christ has issued a set of blueprints, but we must first be open to what those blueprints would have us build. From that openness to build anew comes the rest: the vision, the decision to act, and the long, but rewarding, work of building for ourselves a better world under God's guidance.

A brief word about the book's title: the doing of God's will on earth as in heaven is one of the seven things asked for in the Lord's Prayer as preached by Jesus in the Sermon on the Mount. This doing of God's will on earth is not the sole purview of God, however—we as God's children are called to proactively strive to follow God's will for us. As part of this calling, heaven represents a vision or a template for us to follow—that God's will would be done on earth as it already is being done in heaven. Earth is meant to be modeled on heaven, not the other way around. For heaven to be ordered according to this world, with all of its inequity and inequality, would make it something other than heaven. Instead, our current plane of existence is meant to become more heavenly, which must entail the dismantling of those things which inhibit our flourishing: violence, bigotry, addiction, poverty, and more.

These various attendant evils overlap in their deleterious effects, and necessitate yet another of the Lord's Prayer's elements: the deliverance from evil. Yet deliverance from the evil of poverty—and other evils as they intersect with poverty—is something that the church has a historically poor record of, with the idealistic communal sharing of the New Testament church giving way to the socioeconomic hierarchies of the Middle Ages and the colonialism of the Age of Discovery.

Even as Christian abolitionists and labor organizers rose up to combat the evils of chattel slavery and economic exploitation in the nascent United States, many more Christians turned to religious arguments to justify and perpetuate both of those systemic sins. Today, the economic disparities that exist—and the ways they intersect with race, age, and other demographic factors—continue to be deeply rooted obstacles that have been calcified into our economy, inhibiting the sort of human flourishing that comes from not having to worry about where the next week of groceries or the money for a prescribed medication will come from. Deliverance from the evil of this sort of deprivation remains urgent for the very people the church is both constituted of and called to serve.

Recognition of how we got here, and of how deep-seated the economic insecurity of our era truly is, defines chapter 1. Only when the parameters of the problem at hand have been defined and investigated can a viable solution be appreciated; the purpose of the subsequent chapters will be to offer multiple lenses as possible solutions. Two steps that are critical to this process are the reclamation of the Bible as a book of economic justice and an honest evaluation of Western Christian history as falling far short of biblical economic justice. Chapters 2 and 3 will outline the blueprints for a divine economy as handed down to us in the Hebrew Bible/Tanakh and the New Testament, respectively. Chapter 4 explores how those blueprints transitioned into actual practice in the church-influenced economies of European countries and their empires of colonies. Chapter 5 studies this transition as it continued into the United States and its chattel-slavery-based economy. The ways in which the church's historical economic systems influence our contemporary theology may be invisible at first glance, but that makes it all the more important for us to scratch beneath the surface of these commonly held beliefs and understand their origins. Finally, chapters 6 and 7 serve as responses to chapters 4 and 5 by discussing the ways in which our "divine" economies have been intentionally engineered to take from the young, the old, the women, and the people of color, and how we might begin to reengineer an economy that creates genuine equity and equality of opportunity for all.

You will see the titles of most of these chapters make reference to the "divine economy," which holds a double meaning here: firstly, there exists the divine economy as it may exist in the imaginations of the prophets and Jesus of Nazareth when they spoke out on behalf of the poor and oppressed. And second, there exists the divine economy as it is practiced by us on earth whilst we claim God's divine endorsement of our economic systems that encourage wealth-worship and a financial caste system. The first is that which we are called to aspire to as a part of God's will done on earth as in heaven; the second serves human selfishness and greed even as we may claim that it in fact serves God.

This book you are holding is much more than an alarm, ringing out about the dangers of putting the church's imprimatur upon an economy that works for far too few and oppresses many of the rest of us. Because of this reality, this book is not meant to act as a tool-kit of the "contact your elected representatives" variety—although it is important to do so. The church—and religion more broadly—represents a different way of engaging issues of economic justice, and it is my hope that what we talk about here offers tools for changing the paradigm with which US Christianity in particular approaches matters of economics and labor.

To do so, honest and difficult conversations will have to be had, hearts and souls will have to be examined, and guidance from the Holy Spirit must be sought. What this book will do, I hope and pray, is give you the tools to begin those conversations, examinations, and prayers in earnest if you or your faith community has not yet done so, or to give you the encouragement to continue down that sometimes difficult but important path if you have. Because I may not know your local individual or community context, far be it for me tell you exactly what to do. But the "doing" part of being a religious community is vital to many of the topics raised in these pages. Simply raising awareness or bringing about right belief will not do. It never did. We are not saved by right belief alone. As James, the brother of Jesus, famously wrote in his letter that we will talk about, faith without works is dead.

What I can do is give you the tools to offer new understanding and, based on that new understanding, discern what you can and should do next. What we explore here is meant to give you the biblical, historical, theological, and sociological tools to work for change in your own contexts, wherever they may be. In this way, this book is also meant to serve as a blueprint, a manual, and a source of spiritual nourishment and inspiration, especially if you feel like you are having to survive on the ashes this economy has to offer.

For while ashes may not be a literal foodstuff found in any household's pantry, they remain a potent spiritual symbol not only for their connotations of penitence and humbleness, but also for its association with the phoenix of myth and lore. From the ashes of its own self-immolation a phoenix emerged, prepared to live once more in the heat and light of creation. Arising, like the phoenix, from the ashes has become a powerful image that many a writer before me has reached for.

One of those writers was the early-twentieth-century International Workers of the World activist and songsmith Ralph Chaplin, who concluded his immortal pro-union anthem "Solidarity Forever" with the following stanza:

> In our hands is placed a power greater than their hoarded gold
> Greater than the might of armies, multiplied a thousand-fold
> We can bring to birth a new world from the ashes of the old
> For the union makes us strong

For Chaplin, ashes are the crucial ingredient birthing a new world. Newness does not have to issue forth from nothingness; it can also come from what already exists. I believe a new world of justice and equality can indeed spring from the ashes we have been told must sustain us, but we must first rededicate those ashes for such a holy and sacred purpose if our new world is to have any hope of survival. Then, as members of a broader union bound together by the Holy Spirit, we must get to work creating a new world.

That new world will not be brought forth overnight. It will not come about miraculously or accidentally. A new world that values the poor the way we have historically valued the rich, and the laborer the way we have historically valued the owner, can only come about through purpose and great care.

May we, then, strive ever onward toward birthing that new world, to creating it and bringing it forth out of the ashes that we, and our neighbors around the world, have long been expected to labor for in a merciless and soulless economy. May we one day confound the reality that Jeremiah laments, and in its place create a reality that Jeremiah—and God—would celebrate.

This is the hope I have for us.

Vancouver, Washington
July 2018

CHAPTER 1

A Modern-Day Famine
Wealth and Inequality in the Twenty-First Century

My father Gordon looks at me over his seven-week-old granddaughter, whom he is cradling in his arms.

"The goals of unionism and the social teachings of Jesus should be roughly the same, and some of organized labor has intersected with religion, but so too did much of labor move away from organized religion. A lot of the early IWW (International Workers of the World) organizers? They had no real use for religion," he says matter-of-factly.

At the dining table of my modest townhouse in Vancouver, Washington, my dad, currently an appellate judge in Kansas but previously an attorney who represented labor unions for over fifteen years, converses easily on the topic of my doctoral thesis: the intersection of Christian social teaching and labor organizing. Even though the ink on my diploma is still drying, my dad supplements my knowledge of the subject with his years living this history. We cover all sorts of ground in a short amount of time—songsmiths like Woody Guthrie and Ralph Chaplin, the geographic and ethnographic distinctions in how different union locals organized themselves, and much more.

As a judge, my dad is used to communicating in multipage opinions; extracting an elevator-speech sound bite from him is a rare occurrence. But his aside about the eschewing of religion by many labor organizers hangs in my mind. It is a potent reminder that, immersed though I am in the language and trappings of organized Christianity, there continues to be a chasm between my religion and the organizations my father

1

and I believe strive for the social teachings my faith espouses, but it remains as important as ever to work to bridge that chasm.

My father is what I affectionately refer to as a CEO. Not a Chief Executive Officer (that would be a rather incongruous title for a former labor union attorney, after all), but a Christmas and Easter Only churchgoer. But his understanding of the role Christianity has played over the course of the history of the United States is remarkably broad, and I think that going to him for an outside-the-pews perspective on my faith's role in the American story acts as a vital system check for my own worldview. When we look at how we arrived at this moment of stratified wealth unseen since before the Great Depression, a similar vital system check is in order. If the American church—indeed, any organized faith—is going to proactively approach economic inequality, understanding how we got to where we are is of paramount importance.

What Is So Special About Now?

One of my favorite tidbits of church history trivia is that just before the Protestant Reformation began in 1517, the Roman Catholic Church issued a decree through the Fifth Lateran Council banning the preaching of "any fixed time of future evils, of [the] Antichrist's coming, or the day of Last Judgment."[1] That a church council decided that such a decree was necessary suggests that predicting the exact date of the Antichrist's arrival or of the End Times was already a widespread practice, and yet that prohibition has done little to deter the cottage industry that has thrived within Christianity dedicated to predicting the end of the world—with a reliably 100 percent rate of failure.

In spite of this ban, after the Reformation, those apocalyptic predictions, combined with rampant anti-Catholicism, made the papacy one of the most frequently suggested candidates for the Antichrist.

---

1. Jason Boyett, *Pocket Guide to the Apocalypse: The Official Field Manual for the End of the World* (Relevant Media Group, 2005), 34.

But the collective belief of most any generation that they are living in the most important time contributes to our sense of an ending. Throughout the twentieth century, there were predictions that a dictator like Adolf Hitler, and then Josef Stalin, would be the Antichrist. Then the predictions turned to Islamist terrorists, among others. Our predictions for who might usher in the End Times are flexible enough to morph from one generation's bogeyman to the next, because the prediction itself does not actually change that much. Each generation sees themselves living in a moment of unparalleled importance in world history, whether or not they are.

As a general rule, I try to stay away from the "we live in an auspicious moment in history" sort of rhetoric. We may well be living in such a moment, but that assessment is probably best made by future historians. However, I do believe in each generation rising to meet the challenges unique to its particular epoch of time.

The Greatest Generation took on Nazism and European fascism. The generation before theirs had to arrest the Great Depression and the destructive effects of Prohibition. And, among the other challenges like climate change and the reemergence of fascism in the form of far-right governments across Europe, Generation X, Generation Z, and my generation of millennials will have to face down the tide of economic inequality on a scale more massive than anything seen in the United States prior to the Great Depression.

These challenges are not merely economic, diplomatic, or environmental. They are fundamental moral challenges as well, for they concern the basic wellbeing of humanity, and our capacity to flourish within those circumstances. Economic challenges are not limited to dollars and cents. Environmental challenges are not limited to tree hugging and spotted owls. Ecology concerns the very fabric of life, and because God is the author of life, these challenges are inherently theological. They demand a response from the church beyond inexplicably deciding that the environment is not worth sweating over because Jesus might return before the earth runs out of the resources to sustain human life.

I see similarities in the church's limited response to the economic inequities of our post-Great-Recession era. The willingness to punt on the issue, a hastening to justify a person's poverty because of their personal immorality, a misappropriation of scripture to justify wealth-hoarding, are all behaviors that I have seen frequently throughout a decade of parish ministry, and have come to believe are symptoms of a deeper malaise affecting the church. The raison d'etre of this book is not only to try to define and arrest that malaise, but to offer a vision of moral clarity against inequality in response.

To buttress this vision of a church that sees its moral calling in standing against the wage and wealth thefts of the poor by the rich, I cannot rely on anecdotal evidence. Statistics are also needed to underscore the breadth and depth of the present crisis.

Numbers Tell a Story, Too

Back when I was beginning the initial work for this book, news broke that Facebook had experienced one of the worst single-day losses of market value in history. Nearly $120 billion in value was erased. Mark Zuckerberg lost an estimated $11 billion in personal worth.[2]

To put those staggering figures in the context of an ordinary household's income, the $11 billion that Zuckerberg lost in a single day is over 243,000 times higher than my before-taxes annual salary was at my first full-time ministry call. Assuming an active career of forty years, because of its biblical connotations and it represents the time between ages twenty-five and the traditional retirement age of sixty-five, I would have to work 6,075 active careers in ordained ministry to gross what he lost in one day.

That one person would have to work over six thousand lifetimes to earn what another could lose in a single day and still be a billionaire should serve as *prima facie* evidence that our economic system is grievously immoral. I do not think that our economy is broken,

---

2. David P. Gelles, https://twitter.com/gelles/status/1022476401944002560, July 26, 2017, accessed July 27, 2017.

however. I think it is working exactly as it was designed. While I did not get into professional ministry to get rich, neither did I do it to be happy with an economy that lavishly bestows the fatted calves on a select few while the rest are left to content ourselves with the crumbs that fall (or trickle down, as it were) from the table. Our economy is fundamentally unequal, not broken by accident.

The juxtaposition of my personal finances with Zuckerberg's illustrates a fundamental principle that I try to adhere to in ministry: I believe in combining personal experience with statistical data because the two have a symbiotic relationship. Without the data, I cannot place my personal narrative into a wider context, but without the personal stories, it is tempting to see the data only as abstract and impersonal. As with *Oregon Trail Theology*, then, *On Earth as It Is in Heaven* will strive to utilize both narratives and statistics. In order to communicate the sheer dimensions of the golden calf we have created for ourselves, it is necessary to discuss some ghastly, but hopefully reversible, statistics.

In the United States, a stratification of wealth like that of the Gilded Age of the 1910s or the Roaring Twenties has set in: 35 percent of the total net worth of the United States population is owned by the wealthiest 1 percent; 63 percent by the wealthiest 5 percent; 76 percent by the wealthiest 10 percent; 88 percent by the wealthiest 20 percent; and 97 percent by the wealthiest 40 percent;[3] leaving a scarce 3 percent of the nation's wealth for the remaining 60 percent of the population, or nearly two hundred million people.

In the past, labor unions have acted as instruments against this rising tide of wealth inequality, but the union membership rate of the United States workforce for 2015 (the most recent year available as of this writing) sat at only 11.1 percent,[4] well below one-third of the

---

3. Christopher Ingraham, "If You Thought Income Inequality Was Bad, Get a Load of Wealth Inequality," *The Washington Post*, http://www.washingtonpost.com/news/wonk/wp/2015/05/21/the-top-10-of-americans-own-76-of-the-stuff-and-its-dragging-our-economy-down/, May 21, 2015, accessed July 25, 2018.

4. "Union Members Summary," U.S. Bureau of Labor Statistics, http://www.bls.gov/news.release/union2.nr0.htm, January 28, 2016, accessed July 25, 2018.

peak union membership rate of 35 percent during the mid-1950s.[5]
Meanwhile, the minimum wage has failed to keep up with inflation
since its peak value in the year 1968,[6] and the amount of savings for
most individuals in the United States is low—in most cases, less than
$1,000. The rate of saving is approximately half of what it was during
the mid-1960s.[7] Compared to the vast sums held by modern-day
tycoons, these meager savings are the humble ashes of which Jeremiah
speaks when he says that nations collectively labor in vain. The scales
of wealth are not simply tipped to one side or the other. The scale
itself has toppled over from the lopsided weight.

Today this stratification of wealth continues seemingly unabated,
as does the neutralization of institutional bulwarks meant to check
against such stratification ever happening again after the Gilded
Age, Roaring Twenties, and Great Depression. The 60 percent of the
United States population who hold only 3 percent of the wealth risk
losing any voice they may once have had to advocate for their physical
and spiritual needs in the public square and the media.

While physical and spiritual needs do intersect, it is important to
differentiate them here for the purposes of this book. I am a pastor
by vocation; I have been trained in the provision of spiritual care primarily and economic care secondarily. Concern for spiritual need can
overlap into fields such as the sociology of religion to perform studies on the nature of spirituality and economic inequality. However,
sociologists are not pastors, and it is unfair to expect them to function
or think like pastors. Being a pastor offers particular interest and skills
in the practice of spiritual care with which to address and potentially
answer the basic question of how the church can, and should, address
economic inequality in our time.

5. Steven Greenhouse, "Union Membership in U.S. Fell to 70-Year Low Last Year," *The New York Times*, http://www.nytimes.com/2011/01/22/business/22union.html, January 21, 2011, accessed July 25, 2018.

6. Drew DeSilver, "5 Facts about the Minimum Wage," Pew Research Center, http://www.pewresearch.org/fact-tank/2017/01/04/5-facts-about-the-minimum-wage/, January 4, 2017, accessed July 25, 2018.

7. Sean Williams, "Nearly 7 in 10 Americans Have Less Than $1,000 in Savings," *USA Today*, http://www.usatoday.com/story/money/personalfinance/2016/10/09/savings-study/91083712, October 9, 2016, accessed July 25, 2016.

It may be tempting to either view the people I will write about solely as data points in an effort to be as objective as possible (even if full objectivity is an impossible goal) or to romanticize the plight of the laborer and the poor. "David versus Goliath" is a common axiom in the American zeitgeist, as are "heartland values" and the "voices of rural Americans." This book aims to fall into neither trap, and to instead let the data, scripture, and church history speak and give you the space to act and respond as you feel the Holy Spirit encouraging you to do.

With the wind of the Spirit at our backs, let us move forward in plumbing the extent of our modern-day famine, factor by factor.

Education by State and Zip Code

I lead off with education as the first of several factors to exposit in this first chapter because it was the crucible behind one of the strikes that I researched—the Kelso Education Association of schoolteachers went on strike as a part of the statewide wave of schoolteacher strikes in 2015. But Washington State was also replicating a phenomenon I saw out of my home state of Kansas—an intractable unwillingness by elected officials to fund our children's education in an even minimally constitutional manner. As I write these words three years later, schoolteachers across the state once again have been forced to go on strike after being left little option by the state and their school districts.

While I have made my home on the West Coast for my entire adult life, I am a born-and-raised Kansan. I was born in a hospital in Wichita, raised outside of Kansas City, attended Kansas public schools, and formed my Christian faith in a Disciples of Christ congregation located in Kansas. Kansas will always be home to me. Which was why, even after moving away, it was wrenching to read all about the destructive consequences of the state government's grand "tax experiment" over the past decade that slashed income taxes across the board and reduced a key corporate tax rate from 7 percent to 0 percent, leading to an almost immediate 10 percent loss in tax revenue, and subsequently devastating reductions to vital government services, including infrastructure and public schools.[8]

If state budgets are reflections of our society's choices and values, then we are not properly valuing our children or their teachers. Washington is by no means the only state to cope with a teachers' strike over inadequate funding or low pay. Teacher unions called labor actions in Los Angeles, Chicago, Denver, Ohio, West Virginia, Oklahoma, and Arizona, among other areas, in the past few years to draw attention to their collective plight. In my own hometown of Kansas City, decades of white flight out of the city proper have contributed to lopsided underfunding of schools with a higher percentage of students of color, representing a generations-long theft. As an adult, I have come to realize that my own public school education unjustly benefited from such a disparity. My zip code and my home state determined much about the quality of my education.

Most school districts in the United States rely on a combination of state and local funding, along with a relatively small contribution of federal funding. Even if state funding nominally increases or simply remains steady, a loss of local funding can prove devastating for a school district. State funding for public education is neither increasing nor remaining steady; in a majority of states, funding has decreased on a per-student basis since 2008, and local funding has not been able to fill in all the budgetary holes.[9]

As we the people continue to underfund our public schools, the schools have begun to take on qualities of many churches—though perhaps not the qualities of communal prayer and scripture reading as some Christians would hope. Deferred maintenance, crumbling infrastructure, and underpaid staff are now daily parts of life for many schools just as they are with many churches. As a pastor, there is a

8. Jeremy Hobson, Samantha Raphaelson, and Dean Russell, "As Trump Proposes Tax Cuts, Kansas Deals with Aftermath of Experiment," NPR, https://www.npr.org/2017/10/25/560040131/as-trump-proposes-tax-cuts-kansas-deals-with-aftermath-of-experiment, October 25, 2017, accessed August 23, 2018.

9. Michael Leachman, Kathleen Masterson, and Eric Figueroa, "A Punishing Decade for School Funding," Center on Budget and Policy Priorities, https://www.cbpp.org/research/state-budget-and-tax/a-punishing-decade-for-school-funding, November 29, 2017, accessed August 24, 2018.

painful irony in the reality that just as public schoolteachers are being forced to make do with fewer resources, so too is the church that was began by a public teacher in Jesus of Nazareth.

That Jesus was a teacher is a basic premise of all four Gospels. He teaches both large crowds and individual households. He taught through parable, sermon, and aphorism. He was called "rabbi," which means "teacher." Jesus's classroom, like any other, needed supplies: a mustard seed, five loaves, two fishes, bread and wine. His example should call us to advocate for our teachers to have the resources, wages, and benefits they need to do their jobs well.

For at least seven to eight hours a day, five days a week, and nine months a year, our schools are the homes away from home for our children, homes where they can find their place and build themselves up into the sort of loving, thoughtful, and knowledgeable adults we wish for them to become. We must care for our schools as we care for our own homes.

Physical and Spiritual Homelessness

As I was graduating from Seattle University's School of Theology and Ministry in June 2018, *The Seattle Times* exposed an explosive reality about a city already living with overpriced rents and mortgage payments: one in four apartments in Seattle was empty.[10] Meanwhile, Seattle has a crisis of homelessness that, on a per-capita basis, remains one of the largest in the nation, with my own adopted hometown of Portland, Oregon, not far behind.[11] In both cities, rents and home prices are prohibitively high. Landlords are much

---

10. Mike Rosenberg, "Seattle Renters Score Big as Landlords Dangle Freebies to Fill Empty Apartments," *The Seattle Times*, https://www.seattletimes.com/business/real-estate/free-amazon-echo-2-months-free-rent-2500-gift-cards-seattle-apartment-glut-gives-renters-freebies/, June 25, 2018, accessed August 20, 2018. I want to acknowledge that the reporter of this piece sexually harassed his female colleagues and subsequently resigned from *The Seattle Times*. I believe his accusers and recognize that the abuses he committed do not change the reality of the Seattle housing crisis, or the impact of the news when it first dropped.

11. Scott Greenstone, "Is Seattle's Homeless Crisis the Worst in the Country?" *The Seattle Times*, https://www.seattletimes.com/seattle-news/homeless/is-seattles-homeless-crisis-the-worst-in-the-country/, first published January 16, 2018, updated April 26, 2018, accessed August 20, 2018.

more willing to offer a month of free rent rather than an across-the-board rent decrease in order to fill their domiciles.

While Portland and Seattle are relatively large cities, the debate over homelessness is happening in smaller towns as well. One of the biggest ongoing flash points I saw during my ministry in Longview, which combined with the adjacent town of Kelso has population of maybe fifty thousand, was addressing chronic homelessness there. I heard a laundry list of reasons for not ministering with thoughtfulness and compassion to those experiencing homelessness—drugs, irresponsible life choices, an unwillingness to help themselves—that felt devoid of empathy.

It was heartbreaking to watch many of the local politicians talk about the lack of compassion even as they attempted to rezone the area to functionally eliminate homeless shelters. It was heartbreaking to hear support from laypeople and clergy alike for those attempts, creating the sort of vicious feedback loop in which both elected leaders and their constituents feed off of one another's shared animosities toward a disadvantaged population. It was also heartbreaking to see much of that viciousness emanate from within the wider church. We worship an itinerant Messiah who once said, "Foxes have dens, and the birds in the sky have nests, but the Human One has no place to lay his head" (Luke 9:58). That should call to question any of our manufactured moral objections to homelessness. Such attitudes are a testament to the extent to which we are willing to revise Christianity to justify our comfort with injustice.

Our willingness to reshape our faith for comfort's sake lies at the heart of what needs to change within the church. Everything in the chapters that follow is an interpretation, whether of the Bible or of history, that seeks to offer a course correction for how our interpretations of God have replaced God within the church. We no longer worship God as revealed through the scriptures so much as we worship the scriptures. We do not learn from history so much as we revise and reframe history to see what we want to see. That may make our Christianity a comfortable home, but it moves that home from its solid foundation of rock to a foundation of sand. Jesus made clear what happens to the house built on sand. It gets washed away. We are setting ourselves up for spiritual homelessness.

It may not feel that way. We may still attend a church, listen to sermons, do the things Christians typically do to practice our faith. We may not feel homeless. But we are consigning our souls to live out of the spiritual equivalent of cardboard boxes and shopping carts, even as we cast stones at our siblings in Christ who live in such trappings in the physical world. It is a vicious hypocrisy.

Food Deserts and Food Insecurity

You may have lived in a desert without knowing it. You may be living in one right now. Millions of Americans live in deserts right now. I know that sounds like a sensationalized lead-in to a local news story, or perhaps the tagline for Al Gore's next film, but food deserts are where many people live in America, the wealthiest country in the world. For all its riches, the United States inflicts food insecurity on millions of its own people.

According to the United States Department of Agriculture, nearly one in four residents of the United States lives in a food desert, which is defined as being at least a mile away from a grocery store or supermarket in urban areas, and at least ten miles away in rural areas.[12] The primary options for people who live in food deserts are convenience stores and dollar stores, which generally devote their limited shelf space to highly processed, shelf-stable foods that are high in fat, sugar, and salt, rather than healthier staples like fresh fruits and vegetables. Dining options in food deserts similarly include fast food outlets that offer fat-, sugar-, and salt-laden food, but at rock-bottom prices. Inexpensiveness and ubiquity are critical elements to fast food's appeal when one in four Americans do not have convenient access to a grocery store. Towns such as Baldwin, Florida, have taken the radical step of introducing government-owned grocery stores at city hall, where citizens of the town can purchase nutritious food in the

---

12. Marie Gallagher, "USDA Defines Food Deserts," *Nutrition Digest,* American Nutrition Association, vol. 38, no. 2 (2016): americannutritionassociation.org/newsletter/usda-defines-food-deserts/.

absence of traditional supermarkets.[13] For others who live in food deserts across the nation, though the calories are plentiful, the nutrition
is scarce. Despite the ability of a relatively small number of American
farmers and ranchers to feed literally hundreds of millions of people,
the United States is experiencing a very real famine.

The spiritual metaphors here are potentially endless. White American Christianity has glutted itself on the unhealthy calories of religious nationalism and prosperity theology; we will get to those in due
course. We will likewise address the scriptural implications of a church
and a self-styled "Christian nation" who ignore the provisions of food
that Jesus made in the Gospels. For the moment, let us acknowledge
that the wealthiest country in the world is not adequately feeding its
own people.

Part of the rationalizing rhetoric used to dismantle domestic food
aid programs like SNAP and TANF is to say that churches, not the
government, should be the safety net. I want to disabuse us of that
notion right away. Yes, there are wealthy churches that do a great deal
of work to feed the hungry. There are still more wealthy churches that
do not do anywhere near enough, which may be one of the reasons
they remain so wealthy. But those churches are not the majority of ·
congregations in the United States. The median worship attendance
for the average American congregation is eighty, and the majority of
congregations have less than one hundred attendees in Sunday worship.[14] I pastored one such congregation for nearly seven years in
the heart of a lovely but increasingly impoverished town that took
the Great Recession on the chin. Nobody in our congregation was
especially wealthy. Many were food insecure or bordering on homelessness. Even so, the congregation offered a full meal most every Sunday for anyone who was at worship, knowing that a number of folks
would pack up more of that food to take home for dinner that night

---

13. Antonia Noori Farzan, "When a Deep Red Town's Only Grocery Store Closed,
City Hall Opened Its Own Store. Just Don't Call It 'Socialism,'" *Washington Post*, https://
www.washingtonpost.com/nation/2019/11/22/baldwin-florida-food-desert-city-owned-
grocery-store/, first published November 22, 2019, accessed November 25, 2019.

14. David A. Roozen, "American Congregations 2015: Surviving and Thriving,"
Faith Communities Today & Hartford Institute for Religion Research (2015): 3.

or breakfast the next morning. The meal was one of several ministries the parish faithfully performed to respond to the poverty that surrounded us. The efforts our members put into those ministries were positively herculean. To say "Let the churches do it" echoes the flippant obliviousness of "Let them eat cake." Many churches are already doing the work. It is not enough.

Demanding that the poorer churches already addressing food insecurity do even more with what little we have is tantamount to demanding that the poor redistribute their food and money amongst themselves. Those Sunday meals and mission ministries were funded by the tithes that came out of my members' paychecks and fixed incomes. To argue that the church should be the ones to fix food insecurity rather than to tax the multibillionaires who have built their fortunes on the backs of the food insecure is simply morally bankrupt.

None of this should be construed as absolving the church of its biblical and historical mandate to feed and care for the poor. But in an era when the churches that are suffering the most tend not to be the megachurches of the televangelists we love to hate on, but rather the neighborhood church down the street from you that has been quietly providing for your impoverished neighbors for years and decades, "Let the churches do it" cannot be seen as a viable solitary option.

This means that not only must our expectations adapt to this reality, but so too must our religious communities. Congregations and their leaders, both lay and clergy, must address economic inequality and stratification in a way that holds our government officials and institutions accountable. If the bleeding of the most vulnerable among us is to ever be stanched, we must move beyond band-aids to the surgeries and sutures that offer hope and healing.

Medically Induced Bankruptcy

In 2016, a meme declaring that 643,000 Americans go bankrupt every year due to medical expenses went viral on Facebook, prompting the fact-checking website snopes.com to investigate. Snopes found that the figure of 643,000 was probably high, but even conservative estimates said one in four of all personal bankruptcies in the United States was related to medical debt[15]—the most common source of personal bankruptcies.[16]

The total number of personal bankruptcies has fallen dramatically during the last decade, from a peak of nearly 1.6 million in 2010 to just under eight hundred thousand in 2017,[17] a reduction of 50 percent. Two reasons come to mind. One is that 2010 saw the worst aftereffects of the Great Recession, with many areas of the country experiencing double-digit unemployment rates. The second is the passage of the Affordable Care Act, and the corresponding drop in the number of Americans lacking health insurance.

Even with the assistance of the Affordable Care Act, and using the most conservative estimates, 150,000 to 200,000 American households *at a minimum* declare bankruptcy every year because of their medical debt.

Into the breach to mitigate some of the bleeding has been the phenomenon of crowdfunding—raising money from friends, family, and people who hear your story online. For many crowdfunding websites, which typically take a commission from each campaign, fundraisers for medical expenses are their bread and butter. On the crowdfunding website GoFundMe, as many as one in three donation campaigns are for covering medical expenses, and the website's CEO says that medical campaigns account for the highest amount of money raised of any of the site's categories.[18]

---

15. Kim LaCapria, "Do 643,000 Bankruptcies Occur in the U.S. Every Year Due to Medical Bills?" Snopes, https://www.snopes.com/fact-check/643000-bankruptcies-in-the-u-s-every-year-due-to-medical-bills/, first published April 22, 2016, updated January 15, 2018, accessed August 9, 2018.

16. Maurie Backman, "This Is the No. 1 Reason Americans File for Bankruptcy," *USA Today*, https://www.usatoday.com/story/money/personalfinance/2017/05/05/this-is-the-no-1-reason-americans-file-for-bankruptcy/101148136/, May 5, 2017, accessed January 24, 2019.

17. "Bankruptcy Filings Decline Is Smallest in Years," http://www.uscourts.gov/news/2017/10/18/bankruptcy-filings-decline-smallest-years, October 18, 2017, accessed August 9, 2018.

18. Mark Zdechlik, "Go Fund My Doctor Bills: Americans Ask for Help Paying for Healthcare," MPR News, https://www.mprnews.org/story/2018/07/02/health-care-gofundme-crowdfunding-doctor-bills-minn, July 2, 2018, accessed August 16, 2018.

Those numbers should come as a condemnation of an anti-life reality that we are not providing for one another as the Gospels would have us do. That basic healthcare could ever be claimed as a privilege rather than a right in a self-styled "Christian" nation represents a sort of theological and scriptural amnesia endemic to the era in which we live.

For a church that worships a Messiah who offered free healthcare as part of his ministry, alarms should be raised. As much as the church focuses upon the Cross, there is another cross, the equal-armed red cross of medical care, upon which Christ's ministry demands that we focus our attention and resources. Just as Christ's public ministry included the miraculous provision of food in the face of hunger during the feedings of the five thousand and four thousand, that ministry also included the miraculous provision of healthcare in the face of a number of physical maladies.

It is not simply that the healthcare Jesus provided to people suffering from conditions like leprosy and dropsy was miraculous, however. It is also that the healthcare he offered was free of charge. We Christians follow a Messiah who did not condition his miracles on copays and deductibles, but asked only that people follow him. Jesus's public ministry will be discussed in more detail in chapter 3; integrating it here helps to frame this next statistic: according to the Centers for Disease Control and Prevention, 88.1 percent of Americans have a "usual place to go for medical care."[19] That might sound impressive until we consider the inverse: nearly 12 percent, or almost one in eight, Americans have no usual place to go for either routine or urgent medical care. With a population of roughly 325 million people, that translates to 38 million who lack access to basic medical care, even before the question of adequate insurance enters into the equation.

The good news is that we can rise to reach—if never fully meet— Jesus's example, at least in the interim. While ordinary neighborhood churches may lack the resources to fix the crisis of healthcare bankruptcies, there are positive and concrete steps many churches

---

19. "Access to Health Care," Centers for Disease Control and Prevention, https://www.cdc.gov/nchs/fastats/access-to-health-care.htm, May 3, 2017, accessed August 15, 2018.

are already taking. As we will see in the next chapter, some churches with the resources to do so are already tangibly contributing toward the forgiveness of medical debt and the accessibility and affordability of healthcare. Other congregations have taken their activism increasingly public, lobbying elected leaders for the sort of wholesale changes to healthcare that churches by themselves cannot effect. Even then, our task is not yet done: we must use our theological vocabularies to replace a healthcare framework of wealth-worship and profit generation with a Gospel message that has not been sanded away by the twin American idols of extreme individualism and unfettered plutocracy.

The Power of a New Frame

If you have ever changed the frame on a piece of artwork, you know the influence the frame can have on how we perceive the art, both positively and negatively. A well-chosen, high-quality frame can bring a person's attention to the object it is displaying in a way that augments the painting's characteristics. A poorly chosen frame, by the same token, can detract or draw the person's attention away from what the artist might have hoped they would see.

As we close this first chapter, I invite you to consider how finances have been framed in your life—including in your spiritual life. Where are they discussed? Were you taught they are impolite or impolitic conversation? Are they discussed on an individual or a communal level? What about money and wealth does not get discussed? What frames do you and your communities apply to money? We all start from different places in the conversation we are about to have over the next six chapters. My hope is that we can frame wealth inequality from a faith-based perspective.

Doing so will require repentance and reclamation. Repentance for the ways in which the church has enabled and abetted the wealthy and powerful at the expense of the poor. Reclamation of the sacred texts and historical traditions that we have ignored or reinterpreted to suit our own selfish ends. Through these two purposeful acts, we can liberate our economy from the frames that have enslaved and oppressed others on behalf of profit.

What we are called to weigh, then, is the extent to which we value our own comfort—to be blissful in our ignorance and to happily turn our eyes away from that which we prefer not to care about—versus the extent to which we value our own salvation and common humanness. It is the equation that Jesus asked his audience to consider with the parable of Lazarus and the (pointedly anonymous) rich man in Luke 16. The anonymous wealthy man preferred his comfort to his common humanness with Lazarus, and it ultimately cost him his own salvation, even as he begged Father Abraham for relief in the afterlife. His earlier calculus that his innate human connection with Lazarus was not worth the price of parting with even a morsel of his treasure was also a calculus that his salvation was not worth that treasure, either. The rich man had consciously decided from which he believed he had derived the most benefit, and while he may have avoided a temporary financial cost, the spiritual cost to him was great, arguably even infinite.

In the world of speech and debate where I spent my high school and college years, this process of weighing price versus advantage is called a cost-benefit analysis. In these pages, I will be asking you to weigh the costs of your comfort versus the benefits of our collective salvation, and, in so doing, I am asking myself the exact same question about the costs of my own comfort and salvation. In a book that focuses on the intersection of faith and economics, to borrow this bit of economic language and repurpose it is very much on purpose. After all, words can be taken and reclaimed. Their meanings can shift through time and effort. We can, and should, understand cost as something that extends far beyond the financial sphere, and benefits as transcending the realm of material selfishness.

Let's reclaim our holy scriptures, our sacred historical and theological traditions, and the mission of today's church and reframe the conversation over faith and wealth. I cannot promise that such a conversation will be comfortable or even easy. It is neither of those things. What is at stake is far greater than our comfort. The work of reclaiming and reframing is urgent, from underemployment to food insecurity to medical care and bankruptcies, and faithful responses are needed.

This book represents one such response, and should not be seen as the only or definitive word on the matter. Much like the scriptures and the history that we will spend the next few chapters putting into context, I hope that you will likewise place this book into its own context of a broad and vivid tapestry of Christian social teaching on wealth, finances, and the need for a more just and equitable economy. This is a conversation, and mine is simply one voice among it. Yours is as well.

In this holy conversation that we are having, may our works not be limited to our words. May we labor together to reclaim what has been lost, to create what has not yet been created, and to build up, insofar as we are able, the realm of a good and great God here on earth. It is a mighty labor that we are being called to do, one that can fundamentally change the lives of legions of our siblings and neighbors for the better.

Let us begin this divinely inspired labor. Together.

CHAPTER 2

The Divine Economy
in the Law and the Prophets

One of the more common questions I get asked when I meet some-one for the first time is "When did you know you wanted to be a pastor?" I am sure people in other professions get asked the same thing. People appreciate being asked about their passions, and a job that a person enjoys can be one such passion. The most straightfor-ward answer I can give is the story of my telling my aunt at a family get-together when I was nine or ten that I thought I wanted to be a biblical prophet when I grew up.

Seriously.

As I grew older and read my Bible more, I began to realize that being a biblical prophet had some serious drawbacks: the hair-shirt dress code, the locusts-and-honey diet, and the unfortunate tendency to be executed rather than simply fired from your employment when you upset others.

When I was ordained for ministry by my hometown region in the Disciples of Christ, that same aunt asked me if I remembered the conversation many years before. I had. She had as well. Being able to share in that memory, years and years later, is something I continue to cherish.

Through my religious studies—four years of college and six years of seminary—I learned that the prophetic spirit in the Hebrew Bible (or the *Tanakh*, in Hebrew) was not limited to the fifteen books named for the prophets. Concern for the economic as well as spiritual wellbeing of God's children is paramount across the Tanakh.

All of the contributors to the Tanakh ought to be considered prophets. In ancient Israel, prophets functioned as divine spokespeople, intermediaries between God and the nation.[1] But, in the post-Jeremiah exilic era of ancient Israel's history, the prophetic tradition fell into disrepute, and was replaced by retinues of royal advisors.[2] Postexilic prophets such as Malachi would likely have prophesied outside the king's palace, in stark contrast to prophets like Jeremiah, who had substantial interaction with various court officials. But even when a prophet was attached to the royal court, such as Jeremiah, their concern for the working poor remained evident.

Two common denominators of the Tanakh passages chosen for this chapter are a focus on economic justice and fairness, and an uncommon rarity in much of Christian preaching and teaching. The passages gleaned using this criteria are not an exhaustive list. I hope you will take some of the tools and ideas here and apply them to other passages.

I should also add that I would love nothing more than for Christians to shed some of the overly simple lenses through which we often view the Hebrew Bible, particularly the "Jesus is all over the Tanakh" lens and the "Because of Jesus, we aren't bound by the Tanakh" lens. This approach of (mis)using Jesus to diminish the Tanakh does a disservice to both Christianity, which still retains the Tanakh as a part of our sacred texts, and Judaism, which is fundamentally informed by the Tanakh, but interprets it differently than most Christians. Repairing Christianity's exegetical relationship with the Hebrew Bible and its ecumenical relationship with Judaism are moral imperatives which undergird this chapter, and I would be remiss for not mentioning their importance. Judaism has a rich tradition of economic and social justice in its own right, and Christianity can learn from it.

---

1. James Kugel, *The Bible as It Was* (Harvard University Press, 1997), 12.
2. Ibid., 12–13.

Joseph Saves—and Subjugates—Egypt (Genesis 47:13-26)

The people said, "You've saved our lives. If you wish, we will be Pharaoh's slaves." (47:25)

The Joseph saga has been told and retold across entertainment, from a stage musical (*Joseph and the Amazing Technicolor Dreamcoat*), an animated musical (*Joseph: King of Dreams*), and, naturally, a *VeggieTales* episode ("The Ballad of Little Joe"). All of these share some constants in the story: Joseph's traumatic betrayal at the hands of his jealous brothers, his accurate interpretation of peoples' dreams, his ascension to the position of viceroy over all of Egypt as it prepares for the seven-year famine, and his eventual reconciliation with his repentant family.

What is typically not included in these retellings, for rather obvious reasons, is Joseph's management of the seven-year famine, detailed in Genesis 47:13–26. The famine-struck Egyptians grew increasingly desperate, and they began selling off their assets to Joseph in exchange for grain—first silver, then their livestock, and eventually themselves. The people came to Joseph and offered their land and themselves as sharecroppers, to keep from starving. Joseph agreed and provided seed for the people to work the land that now belonged to the crown, in exchange for a 20 percent cut of the grain. The people agreed to become Pharaoh's slaves, and Joseph formalized their agreement into law.

You can see why that part never made it into the movies and musicals. It would not appeal to a modern audience to depict the story's protagonist enslaving the nation he had been entrusted with, yet it is an accurate assessment of what happened. Even after seminary, I had not given serious consideration to this passage until it was brought up by a guest speaker at a Lenten lecture series I helped to organize some years ago. Joseph's story is one that is often told through a particular lens, whether from the pulpit or on the stage.

If we see Joseph's saga as only a story of familial and individual redemption, and disregard the economic and human implications of a people being willing to accept enslavement to survive a seven-year famine, then we do not fully grasp the story.

To see Joseph as a benevolent dictator after his rise to second-in-command in Egypt, fits with the plucky underdog protagonist persona most often presented. He overcame kidnapping, human trafficking, enslavement, and incarceration under false pretenses to rule over one of the most powerful nations at the time. It is the sort of stuff the myth of American individualism thrives on. While the individual and family dynamics of the story matter, they were never the only point. Genesis depicts a Faustian bargain the people of Egypt strike to save their lives, if not their autonomy and dignity.

Bear in mind that farming in the ancient Near East offered nothing near the yield of modern agriculture, in which a relatively small portion of the populace feeds everyone else. Even in the fertile Nile valley, subsistence-level farming was the order of the day. A 20 percent tax-in-kind would have eaten up what little surpluses many farmers would have been able to produce. While they may have grown accustomed to paying the tax during the seven years of plenty, when that 20 percent was saved for the famine, it would have been extremely difficult to try to do so during a famine.

Additionally, the farmers' land no longer belonged to them, but to the Egyptian throne. They could not use it as collateral, and they could not pass it down to their children as an inheritance. In the span of a few years, they went from being relatively independent farmers to being serfs, controlled by the crown and sharecropping to stave off starvation. Though relinquishing ownership of their land may have saved their lives, it came at a devastating economic cost.

Joseph's actions were exploitive, not heroic. They were shrewd, yes, and certainly effective, but exploitative nonetheless. "You have saved our lives," the farmers said. Perhaps, but that is all that Joseph has left them with. They had become Pharaoh's *de facto* slaves. Their exclamation should perhaps be read as acceptance of a status already reached than as an expression of gratitude.

The Year of Jubilee (Leviticus 25:8–55)

You will make the fiftieth year holy, proclaiming freedom throughout the land to all its inhabitants. It will be a Jubilee year for you: each of you must return to your family property and to your extended family. (25:10)

Levitical law gets a bad rap—and I would say unfortunately so—directly because of the public witness of Christians. I do not say that to make light of the ways in which, say, Leviticus 18:22 and 20:13 have been taken out of context by Christians for decades and subsequently weaponized against LGBTQ people. Rather, I say this precisely because such approaches to Leviticus—and to the Tanakh more broadly—have made many Christian interpretations of Levitical law woefully shallow and explicitly harmful to a great many people, LGBTQ persons among them.

Taking Leviticus out of its context cuts in the other direction as well—just as verses like 18:22 and 20:13 are taken to be literally true by homophobic and transphobic Christians, so too is pretty much the rest of Leviticus consigned to the Christian Bible study scrap heap with nary an ounce of consideration of the book's context and aims. This is genuinely a tragedy; a religion whose founder and namesake declared the Levitical law "You must love your neighbor as yourself" from 19:18 to be one of the two most important commandments ought to have a far deeper understanding and respect for the context of that commandment.

So, let us try—for a few pages, at least—to do justice to the context of a seminal Levitical mandate: the Year of Jubilee.

The need for restoration often centers around the number seven in the Tanakh. The seventh day is kept as Sabbath, a holy day of rest. The seventh year is when slaves must be offered their freedom.[3] Leviticus 25 sets aside the seventh year for the land to have its own rest from its agricultural labors, and the fiftieth year was to be consecrated as a Year of Jubilee, because it comes after seven groups of seven years.

---

3. Exodus 21:2

During a Year of Jubilee: outstanding debts were to be forgiven, slaves and prisoners were to be released, and all land was to be returned to its original holders. It was a societal clean slate, meant to avoid the cyclical poverty.

The return of land to its original occupants was not included by happenstance. A crucial characteristic of life under the kings of Israel and Judah was the growth of a landed gentry, an elite minority that possessed the lion's share of resources and land, in contrast to most people, who lived on a subsistence level or were enslaved. The economic disparity had the potential to destabilize the economy of ancient Israel. The word choices in Leviticus 25 suggest the Year of Jubilee was included as a sort of failsafe against such economic instability. Tanakh commentator Baruch J. Schwartz notes that the Hebrew term *deror*, which can be translated as "freedom" (Common English Bible) or "liberty" (New Revised Standard Version), is related to a "term known from Mesopotamia, where it indicates the general release proclaimed occasionally by kings in order to create or restore economic stability."[4]

That concentrating wealth and land in the hands of too few people is inherently destabilizing was evident to the composers and compilers of the Tanakh, but is too often disregarded by people of faith in the twenty-first-century United States. For freedom and liberty to be tangible, economic stability for all the people is vital.

Our collective memory may be short, but, thankfully, the memory of scripture is more long-lasting. We have seen a number of attempts to recreate an economic Jubilee that includes the forgiveness of debts and the restoration of assets. Organizations like R.I.P. Medical Debt, which was started by former debt collectors who had a change of heart and began working to forgive debts rather than collect on them, have partnered with people as famous as John Oliver of *Last Week Tonight*

4. Baruch J. Schwartz, "Leviticus," *The Jewish Study Bible*, Adele Berlin and Marc Zvi Brettler, editors (Oxford University Press, 2004), 270.

and as humble as a psychoanalyst and a retired chemist to purchase household debts for pennies on the dollar and forgive them.[5]

Pathway Church in Wichita, Kansas, where I was born, offered a congregational template for Jubilee by buying and then forgiving $2.2 million of medical debts for roughly sixteen hundred people as a part of their Easter 2019 celebration.[6] Such a good work may be doable for a megachurch with Pathway's resources, but what about smaller congregations that may struggle simply to keep the lights on? A step in the right direction would be to understand the Year of Jubilee as not a one-off, but a system intended to occur regularly. The Year of Jubilee was designed not so one isolated generation, but so that all generations, would experience liberation from the bondage of financial insecurity.

The Year of Jubilee is framed in Leviticus 25 not only a forgiveness of debts but also a release of slaves and indentured servants, and a return of land to its original holders. Land could likewise be lost to indebtedness by being put up as collateral or violently confiscated. Because of this, our modern efforts to recreate this biblical mandate are mostly piecemeal. But discussion of a wider Jubilee that values financial security for families across generations must be on the table in parish halls and city halls alike.

The story of Naboth's vineyard in 1 Kings 21 is a biblical case study on the importance of maintaining family land. King Ahab coveted the vineyard, which was adjacent to the palace. Ahab offered to replace Naboth's vineyard, or to buy it outright, but Naboth replied, "LORD forbid that I give you my family inheritance!" He characterized the vineyard not as his, but as his family's, handed down from generation to generation, which fits with the understanding throughout the Tanakh of land belonging not to individuals, but families, and, ultimately, on loan from God who created it to begin with. Ahab was willing to do whatever it took

---

5. Sharon Otterman, "2 New Yorkers Erased $1.5 Million in Medical Debt for Hundreds of Strangers," *The New York Times*, https://www.nytimes.com/2018/12/05/nyregion/medical-debt-charity-ny.html, December 5, 2018, accessed December 7, 2018.

6. Kim Avery, "Church Pays Medical Debts for 1,600 Kansans," *KGGF Radio*, http://kggfradio.com/local-news/437017, April 2019, accessed May 8, 2019.

to get the vineyard. He cast aside the precepts of Leviticus 25 and the Year of Jubilee to satisfy his selfish wants and desires, and God, through the prophet Elijah, condemned him for it. Many commentators agree that there is no ironclad evidence that the Year of Jubilee was practiced widespread in ancient Israel, and it is easy to see why: it directly inhibits the large-scale accumulation of land and wealth, which defined the ruling elite class.

Today, adherence to the spirit of the Year of Jubilee represents a direct threat to the economic interests of the One Percent. The forgiveness of debts represents a direct threat to many predatory pursuits, from payday lending to subprime mortgages. And implementation of the mandate to return land to its original holders would entail the removal of the United States as we understand it in deference to the indigenous peoples of North America. Even if we are not among the One Percent, we still benefit from centuries of wealth redistribution away from certain peoples and toward others.

This landed gentry in ancient Israel emerged over centuries despite the mandate of the Year of Jubilee. With the concentration of land in the hands of a select few rather than the original families, ancient Israel gradually shifted from a subsistence-based economy to a market economy, with disastrous results for the commoners. Tanakh scholar D.N. Premnath observes, "With the rise of market economy . . . Labor, which was once considered as a social obligation, becomes a commodity, an abstract quantity to be offered for sale in the market."[7] Eventually, the kings of Israel and Judah conscripted labor for their various projects, cutting out the sale of labor in the market altogether.

---

7. D.N. Premnath, *Eighth Century Prophets: A Social Analysis* (Chalice Press, 2003), 11.

The Rise and Fall of a Kingdom's Chief Slave Overseer (1 Kings 11–12)

Now Jeroboam was a strong and honorable man. Solomon saw how well this youth did his work. So he appointed him over all the work gang of Joseph's house. (11:28)

At first glance, the story of Jeroboam's revolt against Solomon's son and heir Rehoboam may appear to be a tale of palace intrigue and eventual idolatry, with the upstart Jeroboam becoming king, crafting two golden calves to present to his northern kingdom of Israel as their new gods, and being condemned by an anonymous prophet for doing so. Jeroboam was not just any upstart, though. He had been identified as a young man for his gifts and talents and went on to serve as the unified kingdom's head of forced labor. He fell out of favor with Solomon when the prophet Ahijah prophesied that Jeroboam would inherit ten of the twelve tribes of Israel as king. After Solomon attempted to have Jeroboam assassinated, Jeroboam fled to Egypt and remained there until Solomon died.

This forced labor that Jeroboam oversaw grew out of families losing their ancestral land from the families that would otherwise keep and utilize it for their own livelihoods. Though the Year of Jubilee was designed to prevent such a land grab, land theft was repeatedly and systemically used by Hebrew kings as a way to create a supply of forced labor for the wealthy elite. This conscripted workforce was called the *corvee*. Solomon began utilizing the corvee for his building projects, including the first Jerusalem temple. The corvee functioned as a means for "the state's dominant class (to) provide for its security and luxury . . . (Meanwhile) agricultural production suffers because the peasants expend their energies in military service and forced labor."[8]

By instituting the corvee, Solomon added to the stratification of wealth that had taken place through the concentration of landed

---

8. Ibid., 16.

wealth in a small economic and political elite. Once permanently sep-
arated from their familial land, the only remaining means to generate their own income for a peasant was their labor. When Rehoboam
took the throne of Judah, he made the corvée even weightier and
more painful on those conscripted to work than it already had been
under his father, Solomon. As far as Solomon had fallen in God's sight
by the end of his reign, Rehoboam was determined to fall even farther.

Jeroboam experienced his own fall as he created two golden calves,
declared them to be his kingdom's gods, and called the people of the
northern kingdom of Israel to worship them. While Jeroboam's words
and the imagery of the golden calves purposefully harken back to Aaron's creation of the golden calf at Sinai in Exodus, they also create a
thematic similarity between Jeroboam and Rehoboam. Each monarch
expected their respective kingdoms to follow his pursuit of worldly
wealth. Rehoboam demanded more labor from his subjects; Jeroboam
demanded that his subjects worship a graven image made of gold.

As a general rule, I am hesitant to read the United States into the
Bible. It is anachronistic at best, and risks erasing the ancient Israelite
narrative. However, the image of a former enslaver calling his subjects
to worship gold is close to the core of the story of the United States
and our fundamentally exploitative economy. The United States, with
its own history of government-sponsored slavery and wealth-worship,
could choose to heed the cautionary tale of Jeroboam's rise and fall.
The church's role in this aspect of United States history is in many
ways the heart of this book. We in the American church have enabled
one Jeroboam after another, to the extent that wealth-worship is by
no means checked at our sanctuary doors. On the contrary, wealth-
worship is preached from our pulpits, taught in our Bible studies, and
talked up by Christian pundits on television and social media, from
encouraging the adoration of the rich for no other discernible reason
than their wealth to explicitly repeating pro-rich talking points in the
political arena. But the systemic exploitation of labor within an economy of wealth-worship, while quintessentially American, is as old as
the Tanakh. It can be traced as far back as three thousand years or
more, as can the prophetic calls for justice and repentance.

Woe to King Jehoiakim (Jeremiah 22:13–23)

How terrible for Jehoiakim, who builds his house with corruption and his upper chambers with injustice, working his countrymen for nothing, refusing to give them their wages. (22:13)

Jeremiah is typically seen as an exilic-era prophet—someone whose public ministry overlapped with the Israelite exile in Babylon. Because the prophets of the Tanakh are often in direct conversation with the events and rulers of their time and place, they are also fundamentally reactive, and therefore products of their context. So it also was with Jeremiah. In the lead-up to the pair of invasions of Judah by Babylonian king Nebuchadnezzar II, Jeremiah vociferously opposed the series of ineffective and corrupt kings who succeeded Josiah, who had initiated the Deuteronomistic reforms that made him the final righteous king of Judah.

One of those ineffective and corrupt kings was Jehoiakim (also called Eliakim), who was appointed king of Judah by the Egyptian pharaoh Neco.[9] By installing his choice on the throne in Jerusalem, Neco received a sizable tribute, which came from Jehoiakim's extortion of the people of Judah.

The very first word of verse 13 indicates what the listener is meant to take away from Jeremiah's stem-winder against Jehoiakim: woefulness and a sense of impending judgment for the king of Judah. As Tanakh professor Marvin A. Sweeney points out, the Hebrew word *hoy* ". . . is best translated as 'Woe!' The exclamation frequently appears in prophetic oracles of judgment,"[10] and so is not a term used solely by Jeremiah.[11] Jeremiah's bill of particulars is scathing, and specifies why woe is due to Jehoiakim. The king of Judah has built up riches through unpaid labor, cared only for unjust gain, and

---

9. 2 Kings 23:34–35

10. Marvin A. Sweeney, "Jeremiah," *The Jewish Study Bible,* Adele Berlin and Marc Zvi Brettler, editors (Oxford University Press, 2004), 970–71.

11. Christian audiences should be keen to recall that in the Sermon on the Plain in Luke 6, Jesus balances his trio of blessings with a trio of woes, the first of which is a woe pronounced upon the wealthy.

oppressed his subjects. In English, the prophet's critique is blister-
ing. But in Hebrew, it is even more emphatic. Jeremiah's charge that
Jehoiakim has built his house with unfairness "is a pun on the term
'bayit,' which refers to 'house' or 'dynasty,' and may recall images of
Solomon's self-indulgence in taking thirteen years to build his own
palace."[12] The pun is that while the "house of Jehoiakim" referred
to the dynasty he had secured through his tribute to the pharaoh, it
hearkened back to Solomon's palace, where Jehoiakim likely lived. It
was built by a conscripted workforce, the corvee. Jeremiah accused
Jehoiakim of utilizing the corvee to gild his own dwelling.

Jeremiah was not alone among the exilic-era prophets in his judg-
ments. Habakkuk conveyed God's condemnation of similar behavior: "Doom to the one who multiples what doesn't belong to him
. . . pity the one building a city with bloodshed and founding a
village with injustice."[13] As Jeremiah lamented, "People labor in
vain; nations toil for nothing but ashes,"[14] so too does God issue
a nearly identical lament to Habakkuk, "People grow weary from
making just enough fire; nations become tired for nothing."[15] The
weariness of subsistence-level existence affects not just humanity,
but God as well.

Jeremiah's broadside, then, should be understood not as the singular concern of one person, but the highlighting of a pattern of
exploitation over time that was noticed by multiple people. His warning comes full circle over the course of a few hundred years. Just as
Judah in its divided state came into being through oppressive economic practices, it would meet its end at the hands of Nebuchadnezzar II amid still more oppressive economic practices. This should be
a takeaway for churches, businesses, and governments today: actions
that impoverish people have a dramatic cost for those in power as well.

"'[Josiah] defended the rights of the poor and needy; then it
went well. Isn't that what it means to know me?' declares the Lord,"

---

12. Ibid., 971.
13. Habakkuk 2:6–14
14. Jeremiah 51:58
15. Habakkuk 2:13

Jeremiah said.[16] Even if it does not feel like we, individually, are playing for the sort of stakes the heirs of Josiah were in ancient Judah, we are on a collective and systematic level. The importance of defending the rights of the poor and needy, and in avoiding the buildup of wealth on the backs of unpaid and underpaid workers, demands collective and systematic solutions. We cannot be content with making, in Habakkuk's words, "just enough fire" to survive. We can decide to work toward such solutions in our places of worship, our communities, and our governments—or we can watch the economic decline of the world around us, just as the kings of Judah did in the waning decades of their kingdom.

Jeremiah has laid down the divine gauntlet for Jehoiakim and, by extension, for each of us who have profited off of the exploitation of the poor. He has put forth the consequences of woe that await those of us who fail to heed God's affinity for people experiencing poverty.

For Jehoiakim, that consequence was Nebuchadnezzar II invading Judah around 597 BCE and installing Zedekiah, a pro-Babylonian client king. A decade later, when Zedekiah ended his pro-Babylonian stance and allied with Egypt, Nebuchadnezzar invaded Judah a second time, sacked Jerusalem, destroyed Solomon's temple, and erased the kingdom as a political entity.

The next move is ours.

The True Sin of Sodom (Ezekiel 16:44–50)

"This is the sin of your sister Sodom: She and her daughters were proud, had plenty to eat, and enjoyed peace and prosperity; but she didn't help the poor and the needy." (16:49)

Much like the "clobber verses" in Leviticus, the story of Sodom and Gomorrah has a painful and terrible history of Christian misuse against, and abuse of, LGBTQ people. As many more progressive and LGBTQ-affirming pastors, rabbis, and Bible scholars are quick to point out, however, this story from Genesis is not about

---

16. Jeremiah 22:16

homosexuality (especially in the contemporary understanding of sexual orientation and identity), but about norms surrounding hospitality and consensualness. And concerning the former topic, we are apt to point toward this passage in the middle of the book of the prophet Ezekiel.

Ezekiel, like Jeremiah, is an exilic-era prophet who had to process the collective trauma of conquest and exile. Ezekiel, however, went about the endeavor quite differently from Jeremiah. His series of visions are full of dramatic allegory, and a number of Bible scholars believe that, like other prophets such as Isaiah or Daniel, not all of the visions attributed to Ezekiel necessarily originated with the historical prophet. Like Daniel, Ezekiel had a substantial influence on later apocalyptic writers like John of Patmos, who refers to Ezekiel's Gog and Magog in Revelation.

The author of Ezekiel was familiar with the Torah, because he references the destruction of Sodom and Gomorrah and interprets it differently than many modern clergy and audiences. To Ezekiel, the cardinal sin of Sodom was not same-sex relationships—and certainly not LGBTQ orientations or identities as we understand them today—but the violent denial of hospitality and the threat of violence to a traveling party. The demand of the Sodomites to sexually assault Lot's party was exactly that—assault—which is not comparable to a loving and consensual relationship.

Violent denial of fundamental human dignity, such as in the case of ancient Sodom, has economic impacts in addition to moral consequences. The overt xenophobia toward Mexican, Central American, and Caribbean immigrants in our time, many of whom are undocumented and form the backbone of American agriculture, is teaching us the same lesson. News reports tell of farm owners unable to find labor to harvest their crops, so they are letting their produce rot, selling their fields, or both[17] because they cannot turn a profit, even if they could nourish empty stomachs.

---

17. Mary Jo Dudley, "These U.S. Industries Can't Work without Illegal Immigrants," *CBS News,* https://www.cbsnews.com/news/illegal-immigrants-us-economy-farm-workers-taxes/, June 27, 2018, accessed December 20, 2018.

This sin of the United States is similar to the sin of Sodom: "[Sodom] and her daughters were proud, had plenty to eat, and enjoyed peace and prosperity; but she didn't help the poor and the needy."[18] The United States possesses an abundance of both pride and food, even after accounting for the crops left to rot in the fields. Prosperity for the wealthiest among us abounds. But where we consistently come up short is in our solidarity with the poor, in no small part because we have manufactured a great many myths about the work ethic of the poor that brand them as undeserving of our help.

More than 3 percent of full-time workers and 12 percent of part-time workers are classified by the Bureau of Labor Statistics as the "working poor."[19] With an estimated full-time workforce of approximately 126 million people, that means nearly 4 million people work full-time and live in poverty. And with an estimated part-time workforce of approximately 27–28 million people, roughly 3.4 million part-time workers are impoverished—a combined total of nearly 7.4 million people that does not even consider any of their dependents, or any people who have been recently laid off or furloughed.

Consider our treatment of these 7.4 million people when reading Ezekiel's indictment of Sodom and Gomorrah. Ezekiel does not stand alone in his condemnation of the pair of cities. Rabbi Danya Ruttenberg, a frequent commentator on topics pertaining to social justice, links Ezekiel's interpretation of the sins of Sodom with subsequent Talmudic tradition:

> The Talmud (Sanhedrin 109a) paints Sodom in even starker terms, suggesting that their selfishness and greed caused them to impose something akin to immigration and travel bans. In one place, the Talmud conjectures that the people of Sodom said to themselves, "Why should we suffer wayfarers, who come to us only to deplete our wealth. Come, let us abolish the practice of traveling in our land." . . . On that same folio in Sanhedrin (109b),

---

18. Ezekiel 16:49

19. "A Profile of the Working Poor, 2016," Bureau of Labor Statistics, https://www.bls.gov/opub/reports/working-poor/2016/home.htm, July 2018, accessed December 20, 2018.

the Talmud posits that the Sodomites developed an elaborate ruse
to exploit the poor under false pretenses. "If a poor man happened
to come there," it reads, "every resident gave him a denar [coin],
upon which he wrote his name, but no bread was given [that is, the
store owners recognized such coins and refused to accept them].
When he died, each came and took back his [denar]."[20]

It is important for Christian audiences to know that the
Talmud represents a conversation of sorts between varying rabbin-
ical authorities, just as the Bible, including the New Testament,
represents a plethora of divinely inspired voices. However, our
theology of the Bible can be very different from the Jewish understanding of the Talmud. Jewish tradition uses the Talmud to better
understand the Tanakh, which is not a practice that has a clear
analogy in Protestantism, especially when so many profess *sola
scriptura*, or "by scripture alone." We should be careful to avoid
superimposing our ways of exegeting scripture on Jewish traditions
of exegeting the Talmud. I take the wisdom from the words of a
rabbi, rather than trying to exegete it on my own.

More broadly, Christian readers should note God's passion for
social justice across the Tanakh. For Ezekiel, unjust actions contribute
mightily to the sinfulness of Sodom and Gomorrah. They, and not
an anachronistic interpretation surrounding LGBTQ relationships,
make Sodom and Gomorrah worthy of the prophet's condemnation.
Ezekiel's stance should make clear to modern audiences that concern
for the poor is not a situational aspect of Western religious ethics. The
story of Sodom and Gomorrah took place hundreds of years prior to
Ezekiel's lifetime. Even if that timespan was elongated across retellings
in oral tradition, Ezekiel took the story's lessons to be long-lasting. So,
then, should we.

---

20. Danya Ruttenberg, "Trump's Washington Reminds This Rabbi of Modern-Day
Sodom," *Forward,* https://forward.com/opinion/370241/trumps-washington-modern-
day-sodom/, April 27, 2017, accessed December 20, 2018.

The Messenger's Testimony (Malachi 3:1–5)

I will draw near to you for judgment. I will be quick to testify against the sorcerers, the adulterers, those swearing falsely, against those who cheat the day laborers out of their wages as well as oppress the widow and the orphan, and against those who brush aside the foreigner and do not revere me, says the LORD of heavenly forces." (3:5)

Malachi is the book that concludes the Tanakh in Christian Bibles—but not necessarily in Jewish Bibles. The *kethuvim*—"writings"—of Psalms, Proverbs, and other books are often at the end of the Tanakh. Malachi is easy to skip over as our Christian fingertips turn to the Gospel of Matthew. This is unfortunate because we need to hear the edge Malachi reserves for people who had forsaken a God who liberated them from false gods, including financial wealth.

While Malachi is generally considered to be a postexilic book, meaning it was composed during the period when ancient Israel was under Persian rule after the end of exile in Babylon, he offers a broader message. The name Malachi means "my messenger," a term the prophet uses to quote God: "I am sending my messenger. . . ."[21] Malachi's name represents a clue for interpreting what follows.

Christians have a habit of seeing "messenger" as a messianic reference in the Tanakh and conclude that it must be referring to Jesus; that is a habit I hope we can kick. It fuels Christian supersessionism—the idea that Christianity is a replacement of Judaism and so "supersedes" it—and, by extension, Christian anti-Semitism. This habit also too narrowly defines the role of the messenger by confining it to Jesus, when "Malachi" can in fact be any messenger. In the absence of any biographical information about the prophet, what if they selected the name Malachi as a pseudonym or pen name to reflect their role as a messenger of God's Word?

There are other scriptural instances of this practice. Barabbas, the man who is loosed by Pontius Pilate in Jesus's stead on Good Friday, may well have been veiled by a pseudonym that served as a similar play

---

21. Malachi 3:1

on words: "Bar" was a familial term that meant "son of" or "descendant of," and "abba" or "abbas," as you may recall from Jesus's plaintive prayer to God at Gethsemane in the Gospel of Mark, means "dad" or "father." Barabbas's name, then, could mean either "son of the Father" (meaning that, like Jesus, he made a claim to messiahship) or "son of a father." In either case, such a pseudonym would afford Barabbas a level of anonymity to our modern ears, and in so doing permit him to serve as a proxy for any among us who might try to benefit unfairly from the whims of a dictatorial prefect such as Pilate. In short, Barabbas can act as a sort of mirror for audiences to reflect ourselves against, even if he did also exist historically.

The possibility of anonymity should likewise be on the table for Malachi. By potentially making themselves anonymous through the use of the name Malachi as a pseudonym, our prophet has left the door open (intentionally or not) for others to likewise serve as messengers. Were this the case, we ourselves are capable of bearing the missive of a God who has seen the ways in which we suppress and oppress one another, and to speak a corrective word on God's behalf in the face of such pain and hurt. While Malachi may often be skipped over by Christian readers, then, we should be paying closer attention, as the prophet's words and name may well be giving us permission to draw near, listen, and then speak out ourselves.

Malachi's final chapter contains a list of those whom the prophet says God will be quick to testify against, including "those who cheat the day laborers out of their wages as well as oppress the widow and the orphan, and against those who brush aside the foreigner." Each of these populations are championed by God against those who would cheat or oppress them, and each merits mention.

The widow, orphan, and foreigner all have specific verses in Levitical law that speak to their interests and well-being. Foreigners and immigrants are specifically protected against being cheated or exploited; they are afforded the same treatment as an Israelite citizen.[22] The rationale for this protection is that the Israelites were once

---

22. Leviticus 19:33–34

foreigners in the land of Egypt, so they should have sympathy for the immigrants in their own society. The book of Ruth is a vivid illustration of this rule in action, for Ruth as both foreigner (a Moabite) and a widow benefits because Boaz, in accordance with Levitical law, leaves grain for her to glean from his fields.

Malachi builds on the groundwork laid by prophets like Jeremiah and Ezekiel, as well as the authors of Leviticus and 1 Kings concerning the wages of laborers. Each of those books highlighted the importance of fairness and justice in ancient economies or communicated the negative consequences of discarding such precepts in economic behavior. Malachi said those who commit systemic economic sins—cheating of workers, oppressing the vulnerable—were in the same category as those who commit personal sexual sins like adultery. While the church has traditionally spoken out vociferously on the latter, our condemnation of the former has been much less consistent.

My hope as we move from the Tanakh to the New Testament is that we can see God's concern, revealed through words handed down and translated across millennia, in each of these passages from the Tanakh, and not dismiss their importance out of hand simply because Christianity also has the New Testament to draw from. We are called to find God's word in the Tanakh as well as in the New Testament, and when we do, it speaks often to matters of economic and social justice.

I purposefully conclude this chapter of our journey together with the words of Malachi, an anonymous and potentially pseudonymous prophet who served as God's messenger. With the name Malachi potentially functioning here as a pseudonym, the prophet leaves the role of messenger open-ended. Malachi's name communicates that there is space enough for you and me to speak God's message in the face of historic inequality. Malachi is one messenger, but as this passage refers to an arriving "messenger of the covenant"[23] in the future, it seems Malachi never intended to be the only messenger.

---

23. Malachi 3:1

Perhaps nine-year-old me was correct after all: maybe each of us is meant to be a messenger and prophet when we grow up. May we serve as messengers of the truth God bears and places in our ears and on our hearts, so that the world might hear of the liberation that God has been handing down for millennia.

CHAPTER 3

The Divine Economy in the Gospels, the Epistles, and Acts of the Apostles

My soul magnifies the Lord
Who is worthy to be praised

One of the most memorable campfire songs of my youth repeats those lines in an echo, not unlike a Taize chant, until it shifts to an exuberant shout, "HOSANNA! BLESSED BE THE ROCK! BLESSED BE THE ROCK OF MY SALVATION!" The first line of the song is drawn from the Magnificat, Mary's song in Luke 1:46–55, which was inspired by Hannah's song of praise to God in 1 Samuel 2, after she had given birth to Samuel.

I am writing these words on a cold morning during Advent, warmed by the fire and the presence of our Jack Russell terrier, Sir Henry. In moments like this, Mary's song echoes like the campfire song of my youth, but moving beyond the repeated lines. For all of us, this might be the season for sales, gift-buying, and stocking-stuffing, but for the Mother of God-Made-Flesh, it was always the season of the exact opposite. "God has pulled the powerful down from their thrones," she sang, which is not the lyric of a demure, porcelain princess who insists on remaining apolitical. Her song was one of both praise and protest. Our treatment of Mary, then, and of her son and his teachings, cannot be sanitized either. Jesus was political. Instead of creating for ourselves a biblical Photoshop app, in which we sand away the radically anti-wealth words and teachings we do not care for from our biblical heroes, let us continue from where we left off at the end of the previous chapter and critically examine what a number of New Testament passages have to say about wealth, poverty, and economic justice.

A Teenaged Mother's Song of Praise: Luke 1:46–55

He has filled the hungry with good things and sent the rich away empty-handed. (1:53)

The reframing of the Advent and Christmas seasons as the ultimate times on the calendar to be a conspicuous consumer must surely go down as one of the greatest efforts specially designed to tug on our heartstrings and loosen our purse strings.

This is not simply a bemoaning of the commercialization of Christmas. No, what makes the Christmas narrative important for our purposes are its embedded themes of economic justice. And woven into the highest-profile Christian holiday in American culture is a message that threatens to subvert much of that commercial culture.

Mary's song, traditionally called the Magnificat, has an antecedent in the Tanakh: the song of Hannah, the mother of the judge and prophet Samuel.[1] Hannah had found herself in a circumstance similar to Rachel, the wife of Jacob and mother of Joseph and Benjamin: though Hannah was loved by her husband Elkanah, she remained childless while Elkanah's other wife, Peninnah, bore a number of children. Yet just as Rachel would go on to give birth to a favored son in Joseph, so too would Hannah with Samuel.

Mary resembles Hannah in that she found favor with the Lord and had not yet borne children. And her song resembles Hannah's. Both begin with praise and rejoicing in God's presence, and both tell of the awesomeness of God's works.

God's mightiness is not described in general terms. Both women sing of God's action on behalf of the poor, the needy, and the lowly

---

1. When noting the similarities between Mary and Hannah, it is important to clarify that it would be both incorrect and harmful to draw the conclusion that Mary's narrative and song somehow supersedes or replaces Hannah's. These are two biblical narratives that can, and should, coexist without the New Testament narrative standing atop the Tanakh narrative.

among us. Just as Hannah sang, "God raises the poor from the dust, lifts up the needy from the garbage pile. God sits them with officials, gives them the seat of honor" (1 Samuel 2:8), so Mary sang, "[God] has filled the hungry with good things and has sent the rich away empty-handed" (Luke 1:53).

Both women lived in lowly social stations as either a married-yet-childless wife (Hannah) or as a divinely pregnant unwed fiancée (Mary). Both women sang of a God whose justice involved the reversal of circumstance, but Mary specifically applied that reversal to economic fortunes: the hungry were filled and the rich made empty-handed.

What if that were the church's Christmas message?

What if the church were to take seriously the economic reversal of which Mary sang?

That for-profit companies competing for our Christmas spending are increasingly visible on matters of social responsibility is an indictment of the church, who has ceded much of our public moral authority to companies who package compassion for profit, and whose fundamental goals differ so vastly from those of Jesus. It is not that companies have no role to play in bringing about a socially and economically just world, but allowing them to take the lead will never bring about a just world. Mary's Magnificat makes clear that in order for there to be a full measure of justice, the wealthy who benefit the most from the windfalls generated by for-profit companies will have to forfeit far more than they presently are.

It is as urgent as ever for the church to be doing the hard work of solidarity with the people who are crushed by our ruthless economic system.

The Lord's Prayer: Matthew 6:1–15

"Give us the bread we need for today." (6:11)

My last semester of seminary, I took a pair of classes from one of my favorite professors, Father Albert Paretsky, a Dominican priest and New Testament scholar. One class focused solely on the Sermon on the Mount in Matthew 5–7. A preacher as well as professor, Father Albert provided me with a lasting image for my own preaching: imagine the sermon as a symmetrical entity, with Jesus's proclamation that he upholds, not abolishes, the Law and the Prophets both early in the sermon (5:17), and again at the Sermon's end (7:12). Everything in between supports his claim in those two verses.

I visualize the sermon's symmetry as an actual mountain, with the slopes rising and falling from the peak of the sermon, the Lord's Prayer. The preamble to the Lord's Prayer—the final approach up that side of the mountain, if you will—includes Jesus's instructions on charity, while the slope down the other side focuses on fasting. Charitable giving, Jesus teaches, should be done so secretly that the left hand does not see the right hand giving the money away, just as fasting should be performed not to bring attention to our personal piety, but as a spiritual discipline. Both practices are a far cry from our culture of public philanthropy of today.

I think there are moments for making one's giving public. As a pastor, I reveal that I tithe because I should not ask any congregation to do something that I am unwilling to do. At a time when trust in the church and the clergy feels at an all-time low, erring on the side of transparency when it comes to money in the church should be the rule, not the exception.

Our finances are transparent to God no matter how much we try to hide them, or show them off, which may be good or bad news, depending on our spirit of generosity. Jesus's words call for some serious self-examination of our spirit of generosity by both society and the church. Jesus did not deliver the Sermon on the Mount to one person; it was intended for a group of people. Collective, not solely individual, generosity must be a part of Christian spirituality.

After the opening line of praise of God, the Lord's Prayer leans into the trust of God's unconditional and immediate generosity: "Give us this day our daily bread, and forgive us our sins." The expectation of God's generosity is explicitly set in the present: give us *this day* our daily bread. Not in some future day, but now. While the concept of daily bread is often spiritualized to refer to religious nourishment, there is no indication that that is the nourishment Jesus was talking about. Given that the passages before and after the Lord's Prayer concern the physical matters of financial giving and fasting, it makes sense to read these words as literal before we see them as metaphorical. The heart of this seminal sermon holds an explicit plea for God to meet the most physical of needs, hunger. As the Body of Christ, ensuring the fulfillment of basic daily sustenance is very much the core of the church's purview. We cannot, and must not, shy away from it.

Giving food away at pantries provided by churches and charities has not proven adequate to alleviate hunger or mitigate poverty. It is naïve at best and cynical at worst to simply believe that our pantries and soup kitchens alone can meet the tremendous need that presently exists. We must be engaged in advocacy for and solidarity with the poor. This is a both-and, not an either-or, imperative. Simply having one or two mission ministries cannot absolve us of our responsibility to advocate, and advocating cannot release us from our responsibility of meeting people and ministering to them where they are.

The request for bread in the Lord's Prayer is followed by a parallel plea for forgiveness. We should not see them as separate needs, but as parallels of each other. We survive physically on bread, and spiritually and relationally on grace and forgiveness. Once again, this is a both-and, not either-or, imperative for the church.

There is a temptation to do so with the Lord's Prayer in particular, since it occupies a prominent spot in many a worship liturgy all by itself. In returning to the mountain metaphor for the Sermon on the Mount, however, the Lord's Prayer as the core and apex relies on the rest of the sermon to inform its context. There is no peak of any mountain without its base and slopes. And I do not think that we can responsibly look at the Lord's Prayer, and its core expectation of physical as well as spiritual provision, without considering the context of charity that leads up to it.

The Rich Man Meets, and Rejects, Jesus: Mark 10:17–31[2]

Jesus looked at him carefully and loved him. He said, "You are lacking one thing. Go, sell what you own, and give the money to the poor. Then you will have treasure in heaven. And come, follow me." (10:21)

Of all the New Testament passages concerning wealth, the story of the rich man confronting Jesus is both one of the most famous and—in my opinion—one of the most frequently misinterpreted.

The contours of the passage begin simply enough: a rich man asks Jesus what he has to do to inherit eternal life. After reprimanding the anonymous man for calling him good when such praise should be reserved for God, Jesus responds with two requirements. First, obey the commandments. The rich man responds that he has kept the commandments since he was a boy. Jesus follows up by saying, "Go, sell what you own, and give the money to the poor. Then you will have treasure in heaven. And come, follow me." The man responds with deep sadness. While he considered the first mandate a cinch, something he had been doing since childhood, the call to sacrifice his wealth to follow Jesus was too much. As Mark tells the story, "He went away saddened, because he had many possessions."

Let us see if the wealthy man can serve as a proxy for audiences, particularly those of wealth and privilege, who are often blessed more by birthright than by merit. The lack of merit in the extreme accumulation of wealth was ingrained in the cultural ethos of the ancient Near East, where the vast majority of people lived at a subsistence level while a very small minority lived as the elites.

Bruce J. Malina, a biblical anthropologist, saw that the people of Jesus's time thought the world's resources were zero-sum—there was a finite amount of resources, and the extreme accumulation of wealth could generate societal dishonor:

---

2. While this passage appears in Matthew 19:16–30 and Luke 18:18–30, for our purposes this section will follow Mark's version of the story.

[T]he honorable person would certainly strive to avoid and prevent the accumulation of capital, since he would see in it a threat
to the community and community balance, rather than a pre-
condition to economic and social improvement. Since all goods
are limited, one who seeks to accumulate capital is necessarily
dishonorable.[3]

Stockpiling material riches has a moral dimension, even if only by
way of cultural mores. The rich man may have upheld the commandments, but he did not uphold his social obligations.

This distinction matters because far from seeing the accumulation of capital as "necessarily dishonorable" (in Malina's words),
the accumulation of capital has been a human pursuit for millennia. Ancient kings like Solomon erected displays of ostentatious
wealth on the backs of the working poor, yet they still held positions of prestige. So too has extraordinary wealth been something
to be celebrated in the United States. Modern titans of technology
and industry from Bill Gates to Warren Buffet to Jeff Bezos are
feted across all manner of media as role models. Some of their fortunes came on the backs of underpaid workers, yet their status as
role models suggests that wealth begets morality. It is not inappro-
priate to see today's One Percent in the anonymous rich man who
grieves being told to separate himself from his wealth. This makes
him a cautionary tale, not a role model.

Mark offers no evidence that the rich man craved earthly power,
but he did want eternal life. In this way, he has much in common
with other rich men Jesus offered as teaching illustrations in parables,
like the wealthy man in Luke 16, who demanded of Abraham that the
beggar Lazarus, who was in heaven, be sent down to ease his discomfort in hell after both of them had died.

In response, Abraham told the rich man that the barrier between
them could not be crossed. The story connects to Jesus's teaching to
his disciples after the rich man went away saddened: it is easier for a

---

3. Bruce J. Malina, *The New Testament World: Insights from Cultural Anthropology* (John
Knox Press, 1981), 83.

camel to pass through the eye of a needle than for a wealthy person to enter the kingdom of God. Wealth blinds us to the riches of relationship with both God and one another. Those consequences are eternal.

The New Testament Church as a Commune: Acts 2:42–47, 4:32–37

They would sell pieces of property and possessions and distribute the proceeds to everyone who needed them. (2:45)

Taking scripture seriously means taking seriously the ethical teachings it contains, even when they inconveniently challenge the ways in which our culture unfairly benefits or privileges us. Though we may take comfort in the passages that appeal to us, we cannot use the Bible as a violence of verses to be unleashed on diverse and underrepresented peoples in their understanding of God.

American Christianity's predominant interpretation of God is almost impossible to divorce from American love of prosperity, even when that prosperity is at odds with the God presented in the New Testament. The twinning of individual wealth and Christianity occurs and reoccurs throughout US history. Yet, the Christian belief in the inerrancy or infallibility of scripture—despite being at ethical odds with this fusion of Americana and Christendom—remains present, despite the recent downturns in religious affiliation among younger generations in particular. Today 35 percent of Protestants (and 30 percent of all US Christians) profess that the Bible is the literal Word of God.[4] The syncretic blending of Christianity and American wealth-worship continues apace despite this literal belief in a series of texts that, across centuries of composition, are unambiguously critical of riches.

Mainstream scholars generally believe that Luke wrote both his Gospel and Acts sometime after the First Jewish-Roman War, which

---

4. Lydia Saad, "Record Few Americans Believe Bible Is Literal Word of God," Gallup, https://news.gallup.com/poll/210704/record-few-americans-believe-bible-literal-word-god.aspx, May 15, 2017, accessed February 15, 2019.

ended in 73 CE. If the events in Acts 2 and 4 took place after the first Pentecost, at least forty years elapsed before Luke wrote Acts. This is rather apropos in the Bible, as forty years represents a theologically significant period of time, but even in functional terms, four decades is plenty of time for a collective nostalgia regarding a particular era to take effect.

A decade-plus of ministry in mainline Christianity continues to teach me how nostalgia can act as a powerful intoxicant. Whether it is hoping for a resurrection of the church of the 1950s or for a restoration of the growth experienced under that one legendary pastor of decades past, many mainline congregations that have been around for decades or centuries find it a difficult practice to respectfully allow the past to remain in the past.

How the past informs us is not a concern limited to the present. Our forebearers struggled with the powerful intoxicant of nostalgia, all the way back to the New Testament. Luke fondly recalled a sort of golden age for the nascent Way (as the Jesus movement referred to themselves in Acts), writing down the stories that had been told to him. The collective memory of the sense of community was so strong that Luke described it twice, two chapters apart, in nearly identical terms. The believers were of one mind and accord, and their togetherness extended to their material holdings. Everyone who owned property sold it and gave the proceeds to disciples to be distributed among the church according to need.

To see a certain degree of nostalgia in Luke's retelling of the early incarnation of the Way is appropriate. But, we cannot write off the practices of the early church as the good old days. Luke did not yearn for a halcyon era gone by, but described a time when genuine material equity was practiced, with all of its attendant glory and difficulty. And as long as the church is going to claim scripture as one of the highest sources of moral and spiritual authority, the church has to come to grips with how it has fallen away from the economic practices of its earliest incarnation, just as the United States as a nation has fallen away from previous commitments to eradicate poverty.

Acts 2 and 4 can offer us a scriptural gut check for the canons we define within the canon. With what explanations do we dismiss the vision of churches living as communal entities with no individual claims to any material property? The earliest followers of Jesus lived out Jesus's command to the rich man to sell everything and share it all. It was, for them, a mandate for all to follow and a way to incarnate the love of God to one another.

In my experience, though, Christians who say they believe that the Bible is either without error or the literal Word of God are just as eager to do hermeneutical somersaults to get out of Jesus's command to the rich man to sell all he owns and give the proceeds to the poor, or to get out of Luke's passages on the socialistic nature of the very early church, as another Christian might be concerning, say, Jesus's teachings about divorce, or about public prayer. The doctrine of inerrancy often only gets us as far as our own deeply held reservations about the genuinely radical nature of the kingdom of God. I would include in this radicality the communal nature of the Way in Acts 2 and 4, and how fundamentally at odds it is with the individual nature of American ideals.

As a result, we end up looking to scripture to affirm our preconceived ideas, all the while claiming *sola scriptura*—by scripture alone can we define our faith—or some similar doctrine. Yet, we are in fact super-sizing individual verses or passages that do not contribute to the overarching totality of the canon as a collection of books pertaining to God's passion for justice.

Put simply: one Bible lesson that gets cited over and over may not add to the totality of the Bible's overarching message while another, less frequently cited passage, does.[5]

This overarching message of justice—including, but not limited to, economic and social justice—is one that gets carried on from the Gospels and Acts into the Epistles, including the one bearing the name of one of Jesus's younger brothers, James.

5. Eric Atcheson, "A Hermeneutic of Totality," *The Theophilus Project*, http://revericatcheson .blogspot.com/2015/06/a-hermeneutic-of-totality.html, June 25, 2015, accessed February 8, 2019.

Five Chapters of Warnings: The Letter of James

But you have dishonored the poor. Don't the wealthy make life difficult for you? Aren't they the ones who drag you into court? (2:6)

The Letter of James, traditionally ascribed to the younger brother of Jesus and a leader in the early Jesus movement who was martyred in the mid-60s CE, has suffered from a bad reputation, in Western Protestantism especially. Martin Luther referred to it as "an epistle of straw," and moved it to the end of his New Testament translation to reflect his low opinion.

James represents a challenging ethical word to Christianity, in a manner relatively uncommon within the New Testament. It contains no meditations on the divinity of Christ or reflections on evangelism, and so is out of place in much of what American Protestantism emphasizes. Instead, James contains five chapters of ethical proscriptions that range from governing our words to resisting our anger.

It would be a mistake to see James as a primer on individual behavior. The letter is deeply concerned with how the community behaves toward others, and especially with how the wealthy treat the poor. James sees in this imbalance of regard for poor and rich the corrupting influence of the world—which he places at the end of chapter 3—a direct contradiction with the influence of the Spirit. However, James did not neatly arrange his concerns on poverty and wealth in just one section, but interspersed them throughout the letter. We will study two: the end of chapter 1 and beginning of chapter 2; and the end of chapter 4 and beginning of chapter 5.

Chapter 1 ends with this admonition: "True devotion . . . is this: to care for orphans and widows in their difficulties and to keep the world from contaminating us."[6] James was worried that the temptations of the world would prevent the early Jesus movement from living out what he defined as true devotion; the specifics came from the Levitical laws, which contained explicit provisions for those on the margins like widows and orphans.

---

6. James 1:27.

Two verses prior, in 1:25, James calls for study of the (perfect) law, which he states includes putting into action that which we learn from those studies. Fully understanding the breadth and depth of this exhortation requires a respect for the historical dimension of the Tanakh's condemnations of extreme wealth. The prophets who rebuked the kings of Israel and Judah for their excesses were doing so in a context in which the law's precepts to protect the poor were not being honored. Similarly, James seems acutely aware of the ethical implications of listening to Jesus's interpretation of the law, but not living by it.

A critical aspect to Jesus's interpretation of the law was a reversal of circumstances. In Luke 6, Jesus not only pronounced a blessing on the poor, he pronounced woe on the wealthy. James's letter makes it evident that the early Jesus movement was not living up to the spirit of Jesus's teachings on wealth. A substantial number of Jesus's followers were bestowing favored status upon the wealthy, and James called them to task. "Don't the wealthy make life difficult for you? Aren't they the ones who drag you into court?"[7] lays bare the power differential between wealth and poverty that existed in his time, and that exists in our time as well.

James made the source of resentment toward the very rich explicit: their willingness—eagerness—to wield the socio-political power that came with their wealth as a weapon against those who could not muster similar strength. The story of Naboth and King Ahab that was offered as an illustration in the previous chapter serves as an apt illustration here as well—Ahab, with the power and riches of the crown, ends up willing to accuse Naboth with false charges of blasphemy and sedition in order to take the familial property that Naboth had originally claimed stewardship of. A man of wealth was, in James's words, the one who dragged Naboth into court, and Naboth paid with his life.

Just as Elijah tells Ahab that Naboth's blood indicts him (arguably a hearkening back to God confronting Cain over Abel's murder), so too does James tell his audience that the cries of the hired hands indicted

---

7. James 2:6

their employers (5:4). The condemnatory passage that makes up the end of chapter 4 and the beginning of chapter 5, in stark contrast to the rest of James's letter, is overtly apocalyptic in tone.

Apocalyptic language carries imagery that refers to an expectation of an End Times event that includes some manifestation of divine justice, potentially including the reversal of circumstances for the wealthy, and the poor. James's apocalyptic expectation of divine justice or reversal of circumstance crops up in several places. A warning that we "don't really know about tomorrow. What is your life? You are a mist that appears for only a short while before it vanishes,"[8] underscores the fleeting nature of our time on this earth by emphasizing that we don't know what tomorrow brings. James instructed his readers to say, "If the Lord wills, we will live and do this or that."

"Pay attention, you wealthy people," James beseeched in 5:1, "Weep and moan over the miseries coming upon you!" It is a clear mention of reversal of circumstance as part of a divinely generated order of justice. The clear implication is these miseries were a direct result of their decision to hoard wealth. Humanity was a vanishing mist (4:14), and wealth's fleeting nature was laid out in visceral terms: riches were rotted, moths destroyed fine clothes, and the silver and gold that had been stored away rusted, with the rust serving as evidence of God's indictment.

James followed this guttural litany with, "(The rust) will eat your flesh like fire. Consider the treasure you have hoarded in the last days."[9] There is both a future expectation—flesh eaten like fire—but also a present expectation: the hoarding of treasure. This hoarding is referred to as a past action that has taken place "in the last days."[10] The Greek term James uses for "last," *eschatais*, is where we get the English word "eschatology," which is the belief in some sort of

---

8. James 4:14

9. James 5:3

10. Some English-language translations, such as the New Revised Standard Version, translate this part of James 5:3 as treasure you have hoarded "for the last days," which appears to confer more of a future, rather than present, expectation of the End Times. However, the act of hoarding is still referred to as a past action, which suggests that an imminent End Times world was still expected, and that the wealthy should still react accordingly.

End-Times vision for the world and humanity. His pronouncements echo of Jesus's sermon in Luke 6, where he pronounced woe on the rich who already had their comfort. Coupled with Jesus's blessing upon the poor in 6:20, it is another example of the reversal of circumstances that plays an integral role in James's apocalyptic rhetoric here.

James's apocalyptic language culminated in the cries not just of the hired hands, but the cries of the wages themselves. He personified the wages just enough to grant them the human ability to protest their unjust treatment at the hands of the moneyed classes. The love of money had become an abuse of money, and of the laborers to whom those funds rightfully belonged.

When considering the apocalyptic verses in scripture from Tanakh prophets like Malachi and New Testament epistle writers such as James alike to pay workers a prompt wage, a couple of final advisories and conclusions are in order. First, it is crucial to remember that how the wealthy avoid the prompt paying of wages evolves over time. The institution of the corvée enabled and perpetuated that practice in ancient Israel, just as the institution of chattel slavery enabled and perpetuated that practice in the United States. As with most any ancient-versus-contemporary comparison, the overlap between the two is certainly present, but the practices themselves may not be wholly identical.

Second, while we Protestants especially might look toward scripture at the expense of historical and/or contemporary experience, it is critical not to force scripture to exist in a vacuum. The writers of scripture penned what they did in direct response to the events and divine experiences around them, and as timeless as many of their lessons may be, we must not ignore that our biblical authors are also products of their time. There is perhaps no more obvious need to take that simple but foundational reality into account than John of Patmos's book of Revelation. By itself, the book reads as a vivid and harrowing vision of some alternate reality, and it has been used and misused for centuries to scare people into parting from their families and livelihoods, sometimes with horribly violent consequences. But once even a little of John of Patmos's socioeconomic context is understood, Revelation loses a great deal of its scare factor and becomes a more digestible piece of anti-imperial verbiage, and the famous image of the four horsemen of the apocalypse offers a perfect case study of this phenomenon.

The Four Horsemen's Economic Forecast: Revelation 6:1–8

I heard what sounded like a voice from among the four living creatures. It said, "A quart of wheat for a denarion, and three quarts of barley for a denarion, but don't damage the olive oil and the wine." (6:6)

Look.

I get the knee-jerk reaction to just seeing that I am commentating on Revelation here. I really do.

Revelation is a book that has gotten used and abused for centuries by charlatans and snake oil salespeople dressed up as preachers. Certain that they either know when the end of the world is coming or know that they can convince an awful lot of people when the end of the world is coming, these evangelists and televangelists are responsible for a colossal ledger of spiritual harm and financial exploitation. I have witnessed that sort of manipulation of my family members and congregants alike, and witnessing or experiencing that sort of spiritual abuse can make for a mighty strong aversion to the vivid prose and often violent imagery of Revelation.

So no, I would not blame you for skipping right ahead to the next chapter. But if you stick with me here for a few pages, I think that I can make it worth your while.

As far back as the early church father Irenaeus, it has been traditionally accepted that John of Patmos—whom mainstream scholars take to be someone other than the John who composed the Gospel and Letters of John—wrote Revelation during the reign of the emperor Domitian. The extent of Domitian's persecution is not fully clear, but what is clear from the text is the author's condemnatory attitude toward those communities and churches within the Way who compromised on what the author saw as core aspects of their identity.

He offered vision after vision of apocalyptic expectation, with one of the most famous being the four horsemen of Revelation 6:1–8.

The four horsemen, like many characters in Revelation, serve as metaphors. They represent conquest, violence, poverty, and death. The first three horsemen were assigned icons based on what they represent: a bow and crown, a sword, and a set of scales. The set of scales, combined with the proclamation of the third horseman about the prices of wheat and barley, reveal the economic concerns that at least partially undergird Revelation's animosity toward Domitian.

We know from extrabiblical Roman sources that in 92 CE, Domitian issued an edict halving the number of vineyards in the empire. The edict had a twofold purpose—to protect Italian wine production, and to preserve the empire's grain supply,[11] which suggests problems with the grain supply warranted such a drastic edict. A shortage of grain in the empire at the time of Revelation's composition would explain both the scales and the horseman's exclamation, for both relate to a lack of basic necessities, especially staple foods, compared to the apparent subsidization of relative luxury goods.

The set of scales might be akin to a cash register today—a device to help compute what is owed. The image of a set of weighted scales was meant to evoke a sense of fundamental unfairness. Someone was being taken advantage of. The horseman called out the highly inflated prices for staple crops like wheat and barley, while the more expensive goods of olive oil and wine were protected.

A denarion—the price for a quart of wheat or for three quarters of barley—equated to a day's pay for a common laborer in Israel under Roman occupation. It was not an insignificant sum of money; in Jesus's parable of the Good Samaritan, two denarii bought the beaten man a room and care at a local inn. By the time of Domitian, some fifty to sixty years after Jesus's public ministry, it did not go as far in the increasingly exploitative trade system of the Roman empire. According to Catherine Gunsalus Gonzalez and Justo Gonzalez, "Normally,

---

11. James Grout, "Wine and Rome," *Encyclopedia Romana*, http://penelope.uchicago.edu/~grout/encyclopaedia_romana/wine/wine.html, date not given, accessed January 14, 2019.

a denarius would have bought 12 quarts of wheat or 24 quarts of barley—a grain that was considered of lesser quality. Thus [Revelation 6:5–6] is an ironic protest against a system of trade that produced an inflationary rate of 1,200 percent in the price of wheat and 800 percent in the case of barley."[12] The prices of luxury goods like olive oil and wine were not altered, reflecting an economic system that valued the desires of the wealthy over the basic need of the poor.

What Christians often interpret as a futuristic apocalypse was a commentary on the present day for John of Patmos. We err when we consign Revelation to the future or, even worse, to a specific script about the future that we have written for ourselves. Revelation has been misused to support violent, anti-Semitic, and Islamophobic interpretations of the End Times, and misappropriated to take advantage of people's willingness to give sacrificially and financially. It is a text that opposed compromise and condemned an economic system that punished and impoverished the vast majority of the people.

A common thread of the condemnation of economic exploitation runs from the beginning of the Tanakh to the end of the New Testament. They should be read in parallel. Just as Malachi denounced cheating of workers out of their wages, so John of Patmos rebuked the ways the people of his time were being cheated by the economy. Reading both testaments with new eyes might create a renewed respect for economic justice in the church.

These are mighty and monumental tasks—the rereading of entire testaments, and the reordering of a creation that has fallen into the sin of systemic injustice. Our new vision begins with action steps as small as critically examining the sources and authors of the Bible studies your congregation or denomination uses. Who wrote the commentaries in your study Bibles? What are their socioeconomic backgrounds? How many Bible scholars of color, or female, LGBTQ, from the global south, or outside of your denomination are you and your church reading? How many of them are pushing you to consider the narratives of a social or economic demographic other than your

---

12. Catherine Gunsalus Gonzalez and Justo L. Gonzalez, *Revelation* (Westminster John Knox Press, 1997), 49.

own? Do they interpret the Bible from a perspective of liberation? Does their focus move from individual sin to include systemic and systematic sin? Are you being exposed to voices who challenge you to see injustice on a collective, rather than individual, level?

A spiritual audit of your, or your church's, educational resources may be controversial or exhausting, but I have found it to be one of the most important antidotes to a spirituality lacking in diversity and broader experience. Not only does it broaden our outlook, it also supports the vital witness others are making to and within the Body of Christ. As Father Albert, my New Testament professor from seminary, said, "The sacred writers of Israel knew that we live in a moral universe, one in which we are measured against a God of justice."

Let us settle only for what is just in our actions, in our leaders, in our systems of governance, and in our economics and finances. Until then, may we be unsettled enough to work, and to witness, and to hear the voice of God crying for justice, sometimes through the cries of those around us.

Perhaps, too, we might hear, carried on the wind, the singing voice of an Israelite teenager who has just been told that she and the baby she is carrying are both blessed by God.

My soul magnifies the Lord.

CHAPTER 4

The Divine Economy throughout the History of Western Christianity

I sit in the back of the crowded fellowship hall, live-tweeting an event that my inner historian had been looking forward to for weeks—a series of lectures by Rev. Dr. Daisy Machado, the first Latina pastor ordained in my denomination (the Disciples of Christ). She is professor of church history at Union Theological Seminary in New York City, and she was invited to come speak to a gathering of Pacific Northwest clergy over three days. Back in 2012, live-tweeting was a relatively novel way for me to take notes.

Her lecture series, "Acres of Diamonds: Poverty, the Prosperity Gospel, and the Gospel Imperative," covered not just prosperity theology's effect on American Christianity and how to respond to it, but also how we arrived at a moment in which prosperity theology could gain such traction among the faithful. During one of her lectures, she shares with us that, as part of the patron-driven economy in medieval Europe, wealthy patrons gave their alms to the poor in exchange for the poor praying for the wealthy, because they thought the poor were closer to God than their moneyed benefactors—a very different perspective from the core message of prosperity theology that riches are a sign of God's favor.

The implications of such a view of people experiencing poverty, though seemingly complimentary toward the poor, become increasingly toxic once held under a theological magnifying glass. Equating suffering with holiness historically gave license to oppressors to continue their oppression, under the logic that they were doing their targets a theological favor by sanctifying them. A number of arguments put forth by proslavery and pro-colonial Christians across history come very close to making the same point.

I sit back in my chair, integrating what Professor Machado is telling us with what I have come to know to be true about the arc of Christianity and justice: that whatever the time and space, we have proven endlessly inventive at theologically justifying not doing enough to address inequity.

Whatever the importance of scripture the church may espouse today, those of us in the church are capable of being masterfully adroit at creating ethics that fit our wants, rather than reconsidering those wants and jettisoning them if they do not comport with what God has taught us is just and ethical. The history of the Western church is laden with examples of this phenomenon, and this chapter covers but a few to help illustrate how we got to the point of having a church that has either stood by or actively enabled the levels of wealth stratification and inequality that exist today.

These several examples that follow are not meant to provide an exhaustive interpretation of the history of the Western church, but are rather offered as illustrations of context in how the church has long played an active role in the economic affairs of nations and peoples—sometimes for good, but very often for ill. Honesty from the church about the latter in particular should be considered a moral imperative, for as we consider what part the church can or should play today in economic justice, recognizing the ill is vitally necessary for the purpose of making amends. Meanwhile, studying the good offers us a crucial template for moving forward in solidarity with those who are impoverished, underpaid, or otherwise exploited for their labor.

May we do so without forcing upon them a transactional holiness to justify their suffering at the hands of our human-made—and hardly divinely ordained—economic systems.

In Rome's Wake: Feudalism and Fiefs

A number of different dates are offered for the fall of the Western Roman Empire and the end of the age of late antiquity. The year 476 CE marks the abdication of the teen-aged figurehead Western Roman Emperor Flavius Romulus Augustus, while 410 CE marked the sack of Rome by the Visigoths—the first time Rome had been sacked in an estimated 786 years. Finally, in 480 CE the final *de jure* Western Roman Emperor, Flavius Julius Nepos, was assassinated while in exile in Eastern Europe.

A variety of barbarian chieftains and tribes rushed to fill the void left by the Western Roman Empire. The Eastern Roman Empire, headquartered in Constantinople—modern-day Istanbul, Turkey— remained extant for nearly another millennium. The rise of the barbarians, and that of the landed nobility that fought in opposition to them, ushered in the early Middle Ages, often known as the Dark Ages.[1] Europe experienced the fallout of the splintering of the once-vast empire, its network for trade, and its vaunted infrastructure: "Trade declined. Money practically disappeared. The only source and expression of wealth was now land."[2] One of the consequences was the establishment of a legal and socioeconomic system for administering and exploiting the paradigm of land as the predominant means of wealth: feudalism.

Feudalism has a number of scholarly definitions,[3] but, in its most basic form, it entailed the owning of land that was then doled out in exchange for services rendered, whether that was working the land

---

1. Except for this singular mention, the term "Dark Ages" will not be used. While Europe certainly experienced certain regressions during this period of history, technological and cultural advancements throughout not only the aforementioned Eastern Roman Empire, but also the newly Islamized Middle East and Northern Africa, made contributions to humanity that continue to this day. To refer to such a period of history as "dark," then, is needlessly pejorative, and so the term "Early Middle Ages" will be used instead to refer to this period between the fall of Rome and the turn of the first millennium.

2. Justo L. Gonzalez, *Church History: An Essential Guide* (Abingdon Press, 1996), 47–48.

3. Like the term "Dark Ages," feudalism can carry particular pejorative or derogatory connotations depending on the context in which it is used, which makes it all the more important to define it clearly and to limit its usage to the historically and geographically appropriate context of Europe during the Middle Ages.

itself, in the case of the peasantry, or often military service, in the case of the nobility. On paper, the way feudalism worked was that royalty assigned parcels of land (fiefs) to members of the nobility (lords) in exchange for their political allegiance and military service. With those fiefs came laborers to work the land—peasants or serfs—who were often permanently tied to the land and, thus, to the lord of the land. The nobility and peasantry made up two of the three "estates," or general populations, of feudal society, with the third estate consisting of the clergy. Clergy often operated with the direct support of members of the royalty or more powerful nobility, or as members of the landed nobility themselves, as Justo L. Gonzalez makes clear: "Many bishops became feudal lords, and participated in the constant and complicated intrigues and warfare just as actively as any other lord."[4]

In reaction to the loss of a highly centralized empire, feudalism emphasized localized allegiances, from the (forced) allegiance of a peasant to the lord to that lord's allegiance, or fealty, to a more powerful lord or monarch. Intertwined with those allegiances were the church and its clergy. Feudalism made for a rigid hierarchy in which power flowed from the top down, and little hope of social mobility, or even economic security, for all but the most extraordinary of cases. Instances of the peasantry rebelling against their subservient, subsistence-level stations resulted in their execution. To reinforce a peasant's disenfranchised economic status required not only the hard power of military and legal coercion, but also the soft power of social customs and codes constructed to keep peasants in their lowly stations.

The economic status of a European peasant was inextricably intertwined with their social status. In a peasant's daily life, there was little separation between the two:

> A German peasant's servility was emphasized every day: when he was forced to work for the lord . . . when he had to pay tolls, taxes, and duties that others were excluded from; when he had to show cringing deference to the powerful lord on horseback and to his family; when he was forced to take his quarrels to the lord

---

4. Ibid., 48.

for decision . . . and when he had to pay his rent *before* (emphasis Wunderli's) providing for the subsistence of his household.[5]

Additionally, these economic hardships were imposed in the context of frequent warfare between lords under feudalism that interrupted economic activity and made it even harder for peasants and traders to eke out livelihoods.

The regressive hierarchy of feudalism gave way to other hierarchies that determined human economic and social value and were foundational to the transatlantic slave trade, sharecropping, and indigenous genocide. Just as peasants were generationally tied to the land under feudalism, so were enslaved Africans forcibly brought to the Americas to be tied generationally to landed owners. In both cases, the church lent its explicit blessing to such orderings of society through sermons on the innate holiness of economic oppression. The church's blessing of feudalism extended beyond sermons to also include artwork and other cultural artifacts.

The Patronage Economy: Hierarchies of Artistic and Religious Activity

Patronage was a highly visible aspect of feudalism. By the end of the Middle Ages, moneyed patrons served as benefactors of the creative professions—artists, bookmakers, and the like.[6] A wealthy patron might support an artist's profession as an intellectual or financial backer of the artist, with the artist in turn depicting their patron in commissioned pieces of religious art, or otherwise permitting the artwork to be an expression of the patron's agency and beliefs.[7]

Patronage did not begin or end with the Middle Ages. Patrons existed in ancient times. During the Roman Empire, the role of patron was integral and important to Roman society and politics.

---

5. Richard Wunderli, *Peasant Fires: The Drummer of Niklashausen* (Indiana University Press, 1992), 31.

6. Holly Flora, "Patronage," *Studies in Iconography* 33 (2012): 207–18, 207.

7. Ibid, 215–16.

The Renaissance saw now-famous works of art created as a result of patronage. Patrons exist today in a variety of forms, from big-ticket donors for artistic endeavors to "crowdfunding" efforts on websites like Patreon and Kickstarter, which help a person raise money for professional endeavors in exchange for a percentage of the monies they raise. While the latter represents at least a partial departure from earlier incarnations of patronage by having the "crowd," rather than an individual or a household, act as the patron of the creative personality, the overlap remains strong enough that the aforementioned Patreon pretty clearly named itself after the patronage system.

The sanctification of poverty in Europe during the Middle Ages must be understood in the framework of patronage. The importance of patronage in Christianity during the Middle Ages was considerable in at least two ways. First, patronage worked as a political system through which ecclesiastical offices could be obtained, bought, sold, or inherited. The appointment of unqualified or underqualified men to church offices was so common a practice by the end of the Middle Ages that a new term was coined for them: "cardinal-nephews," or *cardinalis nepos* in Latin, from which we get the English word "nepotism." Regardless of whether the person seeking an office through ecclesiastical patronage was qualified, who they knew and the resources they had could lead to such an appointment. This limited many offices to those who had the financial means and political and familial connections to compete for them, shutting off the majority of the populace.

Second, the patron-client relationship was one of the more common means for religious art to be produced. Wealthy benefactors funded the efforts of artists who would otherwise have had no source of funding. The art that was produced was integral to communicating Christianity in a time when most of the citizenry was illiterate, and relied on the spoken word and visual imagery in their spiritual experience. In this way, patronage directly funded the religious message communicated by the church and its clergy to the peasantry.

Part of what was communicated was that poverty was sacred, even holy, in the trappings of its society-imposed privations. That message would be especially amplified during particular church seasons. As Richard Wunderli observed, "For many people in medieval Europe, particularly peasants, poverty was the normal condition of their everyday existence. Lent justified and sanctified their misery."[8] The message was spread, in part, by different mendicant orders of friars, monks, and priests who were themselves sworn to poverty and preached on its sanctifying effects. The status of those who begged for alms—including those mendicant orders—was a feature, not a bug, for their financial backers. As Daisy Machado noted, alms to the poor were often given with the understanding—explicit or implicit—that prayers from the impoverished recipient on behalf of the wealthier patron were expected.

As it sometimes is today, charitable giving to people in poverty was not a pure exercise of philanthropy, but reflective of a multiplicity of self-centered motives. Some donors were motivated by seeing themselves reflected in the finished product, whether by having their names attached or by being depicted in the completed piece. For others, philanthropy came from a *noblesse oblige* mentality that, no matter how well-intentioned, was gratingly condescending. While the philanthropic intentions of some patrons may be pure, it is a profound mistake for society and the church to trust such motivational purity in providing for its art and culture. Or, for that matter, in providing for even more basic needs of food, water, and shelter. Such trust is a precious commodity, not to be doled out lightly or cheaply.

Though the United States economy has moved past land as the only common way to accumulate riches, remnants of a theology influenced by feudal economies remain widely taught in Christian orthodoxy. In at least one significant way, the Western church has modeled its interpretation of God on the destructive and dysfunctional lord-peasant relationship: our interpretation of the Cross.

---

8. Ibid., 29

Feudalism's Theological Implications: Lordship and Atonement

None of what we have discussed thus far in this chapter is only "ancient" history. The theology developed during this era continues to be taught across American Christianity, with many of the concepts informed by, or even rooted in, feudalism. The foremost among them are the notions of substitutionary atonement and penal substitution.

Atonement, broadly speaking, is the branch of theology concerning the effect of the Cross and the Resurrection upon humanity's collective relationship with God. Several atonement theories have been taught across church history. Early church fathers taught of a few different ones, most notably the theories of ransom and recapitulation. In the former, Christ's death on the Cross represented a "ransom" (or *lutron* in Greek, when Matthew and Mark quote Jesus referring to his own life) paid by God to the devil or to sin itself for humanity's salvation. But since Jesus was divine as well as human, and could self-resurrect, the devil could not lay permanent claim to the Messiah in death, and God and Christ were able to ransom humanity from the devil for literally nothing.

Recapitulation sees Jesus as the second son of God, the second Adam, who was successful in the total obedience to God's will where Adam had failed. This view is informed by Paul's writings such as 1 Corinthians 15:45, where he said, "The first human, Adam, became a living person, and the last Adam became a spirit that gives life" (implying that Jesus was that last Adam that gives life), and Romans 5:15, where he compared Christ's gift to what Paul saw as Adam's "failure." Jesus was seen as fulfilling the divine hope that God breathed into Adam, but which Adam ultimately fell short of.

Beliefs like the ransom and recapitulation theories were among the primary atonement teachings of the church for the first thousand years of its existence. During the era of European feudalism, over a thousand years after the public ministry of Jesus, Anselm of Canterbury wrote what would become a pivotal work in Western Christian theology, *Cur Deus Homo* ("When God Became Man"). Fusing his Christianity with the socioeconomics of his time, Anselm changed how Western Christianity understood the meaning of the Cross, and in so doing affected how theology was taught to Christians, even young children. Think of how often children are told at church that Jesus died in their place on the Cross, and the breadth of Anselm's impact on the church quickly comes into view.

Anselm's hypothesis was that God functioned like a feudal lord in God's capacity as a divine Lord. This made our connection to God more contractual than relational in nature: a feudal lord who has been wronged by those who served him was due some sort of compensation or punishment to maintain the lord-serf hierarchy. As Marcus Borg and John Dominic Crossan put it, this demand for satisfaction must come "before God can forgive our sins or crimes. Jesus is the price . . . . And because Jesus is provided by God, the system also affirms grace—but only within a legal framework."[9] This atonement theory is typically called the substitution or satisfaction theory.

The prerequisite in Anselm's satisfaction theory that a price must be paid prior to God's forgiveness mirrors the reality of peasants paying what was due to their lords before taking any money to live on for themselves. While proponents of satisfaction or substitutionary atonement may argue that it is life-giving because it removes the penalty of sin from humanity, it only does so by turning God into an agent of economic oppression, which runs counter to the interpretations proffered by the Tanakh and New Testament of a God who is passionately concerned with economic fairness and justice.

The lopsided nature of the lord-serf relationship may highlight the ultimate power disparity between humans and God, but it does not illustrate the God of love depicted by many of the Bible's authors. Nor does it do justice to the repeated biblical depictions of a God who cares immensely about economic fairness and equity. By reinforcing a hierarchal economic ordering as also theological, Anselmian's atonement theory has contributed to poverty and economic injustice.

---

9. Marcus J. Borg and John Dominic Crossan, *The Last Week: What the Gospels Really Teach About Jesus's Final Days in Jerusalem* (Harper San Francisco, 2006), 139.

A church that teaches an interpretation of an economically oppressive God cannot credibly or effectively stand against tangible economic oppression. A God who provides Jesus not to set right the
oppression, but to reinforce an intrinsically exploitative hierarchy, is
a God who can be appropriated for acts of further exploitation. Far
from being a source of liberation, such an interpretation of God is an
accessory to dehumanization.

When the Oppressed Revolt: The Drummer of
Niklashausen and the Pre-Reformation Tumult

The confluence of exploitative economics and the church's politics
was not lost on the European peasantry. Feudalism was the antithe-
sis of an equitable system, and the resentment of the peasantry could
quickly snowball into rebellion. Economic revolts, such as they
were at the time, contained elements of religious fervor. Similarly,
revolts against the church's power were sometimes driven in part by
economic factors, and those lashings out were fueled by explicitly
religious beliefs and rhetoric. One instance was a series of Christian
pilgrimages to the small German town of Niklashausen to hear one
of its street musicians, Hans Behem, preach on behalf of Mary, the
Mother of Jesus, whom Hans had seen in a series of visions.

Richard Wunderli's *Peasant Fires* is the vivid account of this otherwise obscure pre-Reformation German youth who experienced
the visions and interpreted them in a fiercely anticlerical light, and
subsequently tried to lead a peasant revolt in 1476. In the leadup to
Lent that year, Hans, the drummer of Niklashausen, began gaining
followers and alarming the clerical powers that be. While his sermons
and songs have not survived in their totality, stanzas have, including
one vividly violent one, based on an opening litany normally sung in
mass: "Oh God in Heaven, on you we call/*Kyrie Eleison*[10]/Help us
seize our priests and kill them all."[11]

---

10. "Kyrie Eleison" is an old Christian refrain in Greek that is typically translated as
"God, have mercy."

11. Richard Wunderli, *Peasant Fires: The Drummer of Niklashausen* (Indiana University Press, 1992), 90.

Hans Behem's devout anticlericalism likely overlapped with his economic circumstances, and probably those of at least some of his followers. While priests took individual vows of poverty, it was not uncommon in the Middle Ages for their orders to grow wealthy on a collective level, thanks to patronage from wealthy benefactors attracted to monasticism, leading to an "aristocratic largesse" of extravagant gifts that enriched religious orders.[12] This phenomenon prompted the creation of other orders, like the Cistercians, who imposed stricter and more ascetic lifestyles on their members, but the association of the church with wealth was difficult to escape.

The story of Hans Behem had a deeply unhappy ending. He was subjected to what amounted to a show trial, condemned as a heretic, and burned at the stake. Hans was ahead of his time. Roughly forty years later, the Reformation set Europe alight with both theological fervor and sectarian violence. Hans also came after other peasant revolts against the landed nobility, such as the *Jacquerie* revolt of the French peasants in 1358.

The Jacquerie revolt—so-called because members of the French nobility pejoratively referred to peasants as "Jacques" or "Jacques Bonhomme"[13]—was not an organized rebellion based on a set of principles, but an expression of fury by the peasantry at their repression. Already, France was in tumult—it was during the early decades of the Hundred Years' War, and only several years after the bubonic plague had utterly ravaged Europe, the Middle East, and North Africa, when the French peasants began their uprising. Both the revolt and its suppression were brutal. as the peasants tried to rid themselves of their feudal overlords and the nobility fought back with similarly violent resolve.

The history made by the Jacquerie uprising reverberated across time. Famous authors from Charles Dickens to Arthur Conan Doyle alluded to the Jacquerie in their work. Such allusions—even to an

---

12. John Willinsky, The Intellectual Properties of Learning: A Prehistory from Saint Jerome to John Locke (Chicago: University of Chicago Press, 2018), open access final draft, chapter 4, available from https://intellectualproperties.stanford.edu, 3

13. Justine Firnhaber-Baker and Dirk Schoenaers, eds, *The Routledge History Handbook of Medieval Revolt* (Routledge, 2017), 68.

event that had taken place some five centuries earlier—were vivid in their sympathy toward the revolting peasants, but also in their clear discomfort at the peasants' aim to rid themselves of the nobility. The Jacquerie was responsible for a history that was not unlike the histories of Hans Behem and the later radical Reformers of the Lutheran Reformation: bloody and borne of friction arising from socioeconomic circumstances.

While humanity may not necessarily understand the history it is making in the moment, or how history might judge it, humanity nevertheless creates what Richard Wunderli calls an "enchanted world."[14]

To be enchanted is to live your existence in some manner of altered state, which is the ultimate impact of history: altering the state of the present and enabling a different future, whether for better or worse. How these alterations are read after the fact matters. How we read and interpret scripture has had a profound impact on how we talk about matters of economics and labor. The same is true of how we read history, including the histories created by those from religious contexts that no longer accept their socioeconomic poverty.

The rises and falls of the drummer of Niklashausen and the Jacquerie peasants indicate that the Reformation, while remembered predominantly for its theological precepts, was not a purely theological movement. Like much of the theology we have seen so far, the nascent Protestantism of the era was informed by socioeconomic and political factors that fomented in the decades prior to Martin Luther. However, Protestantism would soon both theologically and socioeconomically lend itself to the rapid accumulation of wealth as well.

---

14. "'People do not understand the history they are making,' is a commonplace among historians . . . As participants in our history, we cannot know its outcome or how it will be explained in the future . . . Only future historians can explain us—or misread us. That is to say that we—however attuned to historical time—also must live in an enchanted world." Wunderli, *Peasant Fires*, 171.

High-Wire Speculation: From Feudalism to Mercantilism

During the eras of the Reformation and the Renaissance, new mechanisms for wealth accumulation and the separation of wealth from those who labored to produce it came into being. Many involved the discovery and exploration of the Americas, Africa, Asia, and the Pacific islands—the construction of overseas empires.

In particular, the fading of feudalism made way for mercantilism, a predecessor to the free-market capitalism of today, and particularly market speculation. Under feudalism, wealth was tied up in hereditary land. In mercantilism, wealth was both gained and lost through the high-wire practices of investment and speculation, which were initially—and dramatically—encapsulated in the Dutch tulip mania of the 1630s.

European exploration and exploitation of non-European nations was at a fever pitch by the 1630s. The tulip had been introduced to the Netherlands less than a century prior. As market speculation, with vouchers and IOUs instead of real currency, became a practice, the potential for speculative bubbles around imported exotic goods, like the tulip, grew.

We should not be surprised that a flower so commonplace today was accorded such stature centuries ago. As historian Anne Goldgar points out, "Value is, in the end, a cultural construct, whether we are talking about the value of a painting, the value of a tulip, or the value of a person."[15] I would add that this cultural construct of value has long been informed by both religious and economic considerations. The Calvinist Dutch of the mid-1600s were willing to engage in the new economic mechanism of speculation and created a bubble that had an undeniable impact on the Dutch people.

Michael Pollan describes the effect that tulip mania had on the Dutch citizenry once promissory notes for tulips began to change hands at breathtaking rates, and for increasingly breathtaking prices:

---

15. Anne Goldgar, *Tulipmania: Money, Knowledge, and Honor in the Dutch Golden Age* (University of Chicago Press, 2007), 17.

[T]he connoisseurs and growers who shared a genuine interest in the flowers were joined by legions of newly minted "florists" who couldn't have cared less. These men were speculators who, only days before, had been carpenters and weavers, woodcutters and glassblowers, smiths, cobblers . . . Rushing to get in on the sure thing, these people sold their businesses, mortgaged their homes, and invested their life savings in slips of paper representing future flowers. Predictably, the flood of fresh capital into the market drove prices to bracing new heights. In the space of a month the price of a red-and-yellow striped Gheel ende Root van Leyden leapt from 46 guilders to 515. A bulb of Switsers, a yellow tulip feathered with red, soared from 60 to 1,800 guilders.[16]

It may be hard for us today to imagine tulips as the commodity that drove and burst an economic bubble. But the ways in which Christianity may have enabled it and the changes it augured are what is important here. Pollan posited the religious dimensions in a footnote in *The Botany of Desire*, speculating, "It might also be that, for some of the Calvinist Dutch, financial abandon offered a way to atone for what they felt was the shame of their wealth, the embarrassment of their riches: they were trading their filthy lucre for the pristine beauty of a flower."[17]

The fusion of Christianity with the pursuit and maintenance of material wealth by this point in history is nothing new. Just as Christian theology was fused with feudalistic socioeconomic practices through atonement theory, so was Christian theology fused with mercantilism's own practices through a different sort of atonement—not of Christ upon the cross, but of an acute sense of self-conscious shame over the wealth they had accumulated.

Tulip mania also illustrates the way in which commodities speculation moved wealth away from its traditional connection to land toward a specific practice centered around another relatively small group of people with the resources and status to take advantage of the

---

16. Michael Pollan, *The Botany of Desire* (Random House, 2001), 102.
17. Ibid., 103.

practice. Instead of a hereditary nobility, it was the class of bankers and investors who had sufficient capital to create even more for themselves—or to lose even more.

In this manner, mercantilism was a forerunner to the speculative capitalism of our present era, but it is also a cautionary tale. The God revealed in scripture is not an absentee landlord who approves of the exploitation of the people in their absence. As the exploitation of workers and laborers accumulates alongside the wealth they generate, the God-given moral imperative to remedy such exploitation similarly accumulates—in urgency. For too long, the Christianity exported by Europe and, subsequently, the United States, has celebrated not the God of the oppressed and the laborer, but the God of those who would take unjust advantage of the oppressed.

The Age of Discovery: Adding Colonialism and Exceptionalism to the Economic Mix

Intercontinental military adventurism has long been an integral part of Western Christianity in the public sphere, at least as far back as the preaching of the First Crusade by Pope Urban III in 1095, and the many subsequent Crusades that followed. The mustering of men to spend months journeying to a foreign land to claim and conquer it in the name of God is a painful legacy of Christianity that did not begin with the exploration—and subsequent exploitation—of the Americas, but this is where we turn now on our journey of understanding how a Christianity that has so seldom done right by the economic teachings of its namesake arrived in the contemporary United States.

The post-1492 importation of Europeanness to the Americas was neither compartmental nor limited, and one of the chief imports of the new arrivals was a variety of brands of Christian supremacy. Christopher Columbus claimed the island of Hispaniola in the name of the Spanish Christian monarchs Ferdinand II and Isabella I. Only months prior, they had expelled the Jews of Spain as the culmination of decades of anti-Semitic persecution and decisively defeated the remaining outpost of Muslim Spain in Grenada. Spain became a chief colonizer of the Americas, and in 1494—just two years after Columbus's initial voyage—that role was codified in the Treaty of Tordesillas, which declared a meridian separating Spain's colonial claims from Portugal's. The character of the next centuries of colonization was undertaken with the theological and financial backing of a monarchy-sponsored Christianity.

The English colonization of North America did not begin in earnest for more than century, with the establishment of Jamestown, Virginia, in 1607. The religious beliefs that were brought across the ocean were integral to the eventual religious exceptionalism of what is now the United States. That religious exceptionalism in turn fueled the American exceptionalism that justified the doctrine of Manifest Destiny that was wielded like a cudgel against indigenous peoples across the continent.

The Mayflower in 1620, and the colonization of North America by communities of English Puritans, established a degree of Protestant religious fervor for colonization that had not necessarily been previously present. Ferdinand and Isabella, the Spanish monarchs, were Roman Catholic. This fervor was distinctly apocalyptic, noticeably nationalistic, and fiercely sectarian, relying on interpretations of scripture for the notion of nations like England (and, by extension, its North American colonies) as divinely elect. Adela Yarbro Collins explains, "Truly millenarian readings [of the book of Revelation] revived in radical Puritan circles in the seventeenth century and often included the idea of England as an elect nation. In the nineteenth century, American and British heirs to the apocalyptic Puritan tradition continued to produce . . . apocalyptic interpretations of the American and French revolutions."[18]

The interpretation of contemporary events through an overtly apocalyptic lens should be a recognizable phenomenon for anyone with a passing familiarity with End Times preachers, televangelists,

---

18. Adela Yarbro Collins, "The Book of Revelation," *The Continuum History of Apocalypticism,* Bernard J. McGinn et al., editors (Continuum International Publishing Group, 2003), 214–15.

and hucksters from Hal Lindsey to John Hagee and Jack Van Impe. The peddlers of Second Coming snake oil today come from a line of colonizing theology stretching back centuries that was both sectarian—in that it promoted the idea of a (generally white Protestant) elect surrounded by the non-elect—and apocalyptic trusting in the divine protection or action on behalf of the generally white Protestant elect.

This white Protestant elect would go on to claim a sea-to-sea mandate as the English colonies became the United States. The Doctrine of Discovery—the primarily American belief that colonial powers laying claim to land not originally their own was a legitimate, if not laudable, enterprise—fueled much of the nascent United States' expansion into indigenous lands. (Ever wonder why Lewis and Clark's expedition team was called the Corps of Discovery?) The Doctrine of Discovery was closely associated with other expressions of unlimited United States hegemony over North America, from Manifest Destiny to the Monroe Doctrine, and it was codified into Supreme Court case law in the landmark 1823 case *Johnson v. M'Intosh*, wherein a unanimous Supreme Court held that the Doctrine of Discovery, among other things, prevented the private transfer of land between indigenous and non-indigenous persons.[19] Only eight years later, in 1831, the Trail of Tears began, the forced displacement of Chickasaw, Choctaw, Creek, Cherokee, and Seminole tribes to westward reservations, with thousands of tribespeople perishing en route. These actions, among many others, create a mosaic of anti-indigenous political, military, and economic action whose socioeconomic impacts upon American indigenous peoples have continued to this day.

European colonization was not limited to the Americas. The transatlantic slave trade became an integral component to the colonization of the Americas and to the antebellum economic engine of the United

---

19. Only recently have some American Christian communities begun to genuinely reckon with the economic, cultural, and human damage the Doctrine of Discovery has inflicted. In 2017, the General Assembly of my denomination, the Disciples of Christ, formally voted to rescind and apologize for its promotion of the Doctrine of Discovery, but even this, I believe, represents only an initial step toward amends. That conversation concerning amends will take place in chapter 7.

States. It had the imprimatur of the church as early as the 1400s, when Portugal began colonizing the West African coast. Part of those efforts was a campaign to Christianize enslaved Africans, but they needed ideological justification, according to John Charles Chasteen:

> The Board of Conscience in Lisbon cleared [Christianization] as long as the Portuguese slavers were supposedly "rescuing" the captives of cannibals, or enslaving certified practitioners of human sacrifice, or engaging in some form of certified "just war." In practice, however, such legal distinctions mattered little to slave traders. They bought whoever was for sale.[20]

Fifteen to twenty percent of the Africans kidnapped into slavery died en route to the Americas.[21] Genocide may not have been the primary aim of the slave trade, but the slave trade was most certainly genocidal, and the economic consequences of genocide compounded its cultural, social, and humanitarian consequences.

Across the centuries, the church has both contributed to, and benefited from, the human cost of the economic systems it has existed in, even as the church might have also acted in other ways to mitigate that human cost. Those of us who belong to denominations whose roots can be traced to Europe must do the work to understand how our theological forebearers benefited from the economic systems that propped them up. All of us, regardless of religious identity, must push for a divorce between Christianity and exploitative economies. Whether we demand that divorce as Christians who want better from our own traditions, or as non-Christians who see the harm that Christian hegemony has proven capable of toward other faiths, bringing the full weight of this history to bear is necessary to persuade others that all of us deserve something better.

We must do a far better job of teaching this history. Professors, clergy, and laypeople alike must create and facilitate opportunities for unlearning the revised and idealized versions of history we may

---

20. John Charles Chasteen, *Born in Blood and Fire: A Concise History of Latin America* (W.W. Norton & Company, 2001), 46.

21. Ibid., 46.

have been taught, and learn the historical realities that have gone unaddressed.

Primarily white denominations and congregations face a reckoning in our pews with how we have benefited at the direct expense of others throughout this history, and how our founders and theological giants benefited from the sectarian and economic violence that took place during their eras. For those who have built their own faith identities upon this tumultuous history, it may not be so simple a matter at all. It is not simple, but a lack of simplicity does not beget a lack of urgency. Like Jacob wrestling God, we may come away wounded by wrestling with the history of the church. Yet, like Jacob, we also have the chance to come away with a deeper understanding of what we are called to do, and how to address the human cost inflicted by our past.

The human cost to an economic system is not an issue solely for economists; it is also a subject for theologians, pastors, ethicists, and other religiously and philosophically oriented vocations to address. Historically, as the example of the Board of Conscience in Lisbon demonstrates, the inveighing of religious authorities upon this human cost has very frequently added to, not mitigated or prevented, such negative consequences. Even as the work of Christian abolitionists and humanitarians is celebrated today, our celebrations cannot erase the historical reality of a church structure built to not merely endorse, but to encourage, the continued exploitation of other human beings for socioeconomic benefit. From feudalism onward, the Western church has permitted itself to be influenced less by Christ's example and the words of the prophets, and more by the temporal desires for wealth and status that Satan unsuccessfully tempted Jesus with in the wilderness. Unlike Jesus, the church has proven all too eager to cast its lot in with the seductive promises of the tempter. And it is a history that, as of this writing, has never been well and truly reckoned with in either the predominantly white church or in the United States writ large—although, whether come hell or high water, it one day must.

CHAPTER 5

How We Got Here
Christianity's Pursuit of Wealth in the United States

Fumbling with the key, I unlocked the heavy door that led to my office, immediately saw the pile of mail waiting for me on my desk, and let out a long exhale of breath. Because nearly all of my congregants communicate via e-mail and phone calls, I learned to seldom expect anything personal in my snail mail, except for the occasional thoughtful greeting card or the less-than-thoughtful hate mail.

Atop the pile was an envelope with no return address. I know from experience that is rarely a good sign. I opened it and unfolded the single sheet.

Anger and disdain popped out from the page at me. Because I had publicly advocated for the millworkers in Longview who were striking for the first time in nearly forty years, I was a false teacher and prophet who needed to be reminded that these were already well-paying jobs, and I should focus more on being peaceable, which I took to mean disinterested in the basic needs of humanity.

Naturally, the letter was unsigned.

I exhaled again and realized I had been holding in my breath as I took in the letter's venom. While, occasionally, I kept my less-than-friendly mail as teaching illustrations, this didn't feel like a keeper. The lack of signature and a return address communicated that the writer was not interested in any sort of conversation, and all keeping the letter could do was encourage me to focus unhealthily on its message.

With a flick of the wrist, the letter landed in the circular file where it belonged, and I moved on to the next envelope.

I remember that piece of anonymous hate mail because it was also a window into someone else's psyche—and into the views of a number of others in the community who shared the writer's opinions about the millworkers' strike. Opinions like that the millworkers were ungrateful for daring to ask more from their captains of industry, and that they should simply be content with what they had. In the midst of the stress engendered by a strike, the millworkers could have done without such vitriol, and religious communities ought to be well-positioned to address that need. The role of churches and clergy, for many, is to help make workers docile enough to make concessions to their employers. Christianity is to serve, as Karl Marx said, as the opiate of the masses, and we the clergy as its dealers.

I simply cannot accept such a deployment of my faith. Christianity has often been used to dismiss the fundamental need for dignity in work. Beginning with the arrival of kidnapped Africans as chattel slaves and European settlers as indentured servants, the history of the United States is in no small part a combination of Christian teaching and exploitative economics. If that combination is ever to be truly dismantled, understanding its grip on American history and culture is imperative, beginning with the legacy of colonialism.

Living in Vancouver, Washington means that I live on Chinook tribal land.[1] I do my best to be a polite guest, but I am aware that, even though my matrilineal family immigrated as genocide refugees, I am uninvited. How welcome and polite can a guest can be, no matter their intentions, if they are uninvited? Such was the case for the oft-glorified pilgrims of the Plymouth colony they established in what is now the state of Massachusetts, beginning in the autumn of 1620.

---

1. If you live in North America, you can go to the website native-land.ca to see which indigenous tribes once inhabited the land you presently live on.

White settlers from Europe to North America were often financed by European investors seeking to capitalize on the resources that North American lands and waters had to offer, going back to Christopher Columbus's unwelcome intrusion of Hispaniola in 1492 and his subsequent return to Spain with, among other things, enslaved indigenous people to present to the crown not as people, but as resources.

The economic promise of the Americas brought more Europeans settling across the ocean. Those who could not afford passage indentured themselves in exchange for passage, and agreed to work on behalf of their benefactors for a set number of years.

Those agreements were not the economic, cultural, or moral equivalents of the enslavement of black African and Caribbean peoples. Talking about "Irish slavery" may be in vogue in certain segments of conservative white Christianity, but it is both ahistorical and incendiary to equate the experience of white indentured servants with the experience of those who were kidnapped and sold into, or born and bred solely for, a lifetime of intergenerational slavery because of their skin color—and all in the name of God.

First and Second Great Awakenings

Religion was a part of the colonial mix from the start. The Pilgrims who came to what is now Massachusetts in 1620 brought with them an apocalyptic exceptionalism that marked the colonial endeavor from the start. Each new colony had religious underpinnings that complemented their economic aspirations.

By the time of the First Great Awakening in the mid-1700s, the economies of the colonies along the Atlantic seaboard were varied, but still significantly agrarian. Slavery reigned, even in the north. The wave of abolitionist "free states" did not begin until after the American Revolution was well underway, and the Second Great Awakening began after the ratification of the Constitution.

In many aspects—theologically, culturally, and even socioeconomically—the Second Great Awakening was informed by, and in some ways a response to, the First Great Awakening. The First Great

Awakening was dominated by both Calvinist-inspired preachers like Jonathan Edwards and the Wesleyan namesakes John and Charles Wesley, all of whom contributed to the systematic theologies of mainstream Christianity. The Second Great Awakening gave way to "restorationist" denominations like the Church of Jesus Christ of Latter-Day Saints and the Christian Church (Disciples of Christ)— my own denomination. They emerged, on the frontier, not so much on the basis of doctrine, but rather out of a desire to "restore" the church to its New Testament origins. What that looked like, though, was a matter of debate.

The religious revivalism in both found a variety of ways to excuse the greatest societal sins. While the mostly white preachers preached messages of personal revival to packed sanctuaries and meetinghouses, the economic fortunes of the non-white souls around them were not so similarly bolstered. The Second Great Awakening relied in no small part on a brand of frontier Pentecostalism that varied significantly from the settled churches of the East Coast, and their message spread like wildfire as people pushed further and further westward.

Rather than contrast the two Great Awakenings, let's highlight some of the commonalities to understand American Christianity's economic story. Each Great Awakening reified exploitative socioeconomic aspects of American society.

Both Great Awakenings were overtly influenced by racism and the social and economic trappings of chattel slavery. In both, there were proponents who either sought to reify those unequal economic power structures, or who passively assented to benefiting from those same power structures. Prominent white preachers of the First Great Awakening, like George Whitefield, were slave owners and theological proponents of chattel slavery as an institution. Others, like John and Charles Wesley, were staunch abolitionists. Yet, the vocabulary of slavery was common in sermons delivered by white preachers. John Cotton preached a famous sermon entitled "God's Promise to His Plantation,"[2] which eerily echoed Anselm of

---

2. Matthew Paul Turner, *Our Great Big American God: A Short History of Our Ever-Growing Deity* (Jericho Books, 2014), 20.

Canterbury's understanding of God's relationship to humanity on the basis of another exploitative economic system—simply swap out feudalism for chattel slavery.

Just as the institution of chattel slavery in the United States practiced a punitive mentality, so, too, did the vindictive God of many First Great Awakening preachers. Jonathan Edwards's "Sinners in the Hands of an Angry God" was also a product of the socioeconomic factors of the era, including the punitive economic exploitation of entire peoples who, these preachers hastened to remind their audiences, surely merited God's holy wrath.

The Second Great Awakening had its own backdrop of economic exploitation in an era of exploration and expansion for the United States. The Louisiana Purchase was made two years after the Cane Ridge revival of 1801. Meriwether Lewis and William Clark began to explore the territory soon after. They called themselves the Corps of Discovery, hearkened to the Age of Discovery in which much of the non-European world was colonized for economic benefit by various European powers.

The emphasis on discovery was wedded to the religious language—largely Christian—of manifest destiny, which argued that the United States was a unique nation whose irresistible destiny to conquer the continent of North America. Even as American Christianity began to move away from its Calvinist roots, the irresistibility of its destiny overlapped with the irresistibility of grace. They were the elect of God. This brand of expansionism often overlapped with the spread of slavery, which also benefited from the claim of divine purpose on the part of its proponents. To take that notion of irresistibility and apply it to the image of the United States put the country in the godlike position of creator and maker. Instead of the *imago dei*, the United States became focused on creating the *imago Americana,* giving the expansion and plutocracy white Christianity's imprimatur.

The Second Great Awakening took hold on the frontier. Kentucky and Tennessee were fertile ground for the Stone-Campbell movement of restorationist Christians; Missouri and Illinois were home bases for the restorationist denomination that became the Church of Jesus

Christ of Latter-Day Saints, or Mormons. During the antebellum era, other Christian denominations spun off from established brands for both theological and cultural reasons. Most notable among these were the Southern Baptists in 1845.

These Christian movements did not originate in a vacuum. New church movements were formed alongside of white settlers pushing further and further west, not only to claim indigenous tribal lands, but also to stake out lands where slavery would be legal. The Missouri Compromise of 1820 was a codification of the gains of those maneuvers. Missouri was admitted as a slave state, even as slavery was otherwise banned north of the 36°30' latitude. Because Missouri had been quickly settled by a large number of slaveholders looking to expand the institution of slavery throughout the lands of the Louisiana Purchase, it moved from territory status to statehood in under twenty years.

The expansion of slavery and the extermination of the indigenous people were economic actions as well as militaristic and supremacist ones, and the Christian theologies formed to justify them left profoundly harmful economic legacies.

The Impact of Titans and Robber Barons

To take a peoples' land or freedom is deeply sinful. But such theft of home and liberty was not an end in itself; it also served as a means of vast economic enrichment for a select few. Whether the planter class in the antebellum South, or the expansionist developers in the land grabs of indigenous tribal territories, the expansion under the banners of the Doctrine of Discovery, Manifest Destiny, and the Monroe Doctrine (among others) benefited particular classes of European-Americans. Just as feudalism was structured to benefit the ruling noble and warrior classes, and mercantilism benefitted investors who had the necessary capital to exploit the commodification of basic goods and labor, American capitalism benefitted a relatively small, but consistently wealthy, band of tycoons, robber barons, and titans of industry. And, like feudalism and mercantilism, it facilitated a wealth gap that continues to this day.

The stratification of wealth in our present economy is not a new phenomenon, although the financial divide between the One Percent and the rest of us is more pronounced than in recent decades. The argument that the American economy was shaped to create economic castes is straightforward. The United States may not boast a hereditary nobility in the formal sense of ossified duchies and earldoms, but it created a *de facto* nobility in the late 1800s to early 1900s for the rapid accumulation of vast wealth for a select few who used their wealth to socioeconomically separate themselves and their heirs. Meanwhile, those whose labor helped generate that wealth were left with stagnant wages and disappearing benefits.

Wages and benefits were not given out of magnanimity. Workers had to strike and demonstrate, often at great personal risk, for fair wages and workplace safety laws. Some of these laws have survived, while many others have been defanged or repealed by pliant politicians and judges. Any attempt to raise the minimum wage, or to make benefits more widely available to workers, is often promptly met with widespread opposition from chambers of commerce, business trade groups, pro-management lobbyists, and the politicians whose campaigns are funded by them.

What does all of this have to do with American religious practice? Just as the tycoons bankrolled political campaigns, expecting a certain sort of messaging in return, a similar *quid pro quo* existed when they bankrolled a preacher's ministry.

The Gospel of Individual Morality: When Tycoons Bankroll the Pulpit

Dwight L. Moody was a famous circuit-riding preacher of the nineteenth century whose preaching focused heavily on individual behavior as a means of sanctifying both oneself and God. For Moody, personal holiness came not from acting collectively for the betterment of as many as possible, but by acting individually. Moody compartmentalized God to individual sins and choices, which suited the purposes of the business tycoons of his day. Consequently, many of them were willing to financially back his itinerant preaching.[3]

Moody preached anti-union and anti-work-stoppage sermons that suggested that the way to avoid sin was to work. He argued that avoiding personal sin was more important for workers than their economic livelihood. As a result, many of the sorts of industrialists, captains of business, and tycoons discussed in the previous section were more than happy to bankroll Moody's preaching. His message not only justified capitalistic morality, but also minimized the laborer's lack of financial security. Personal salvation was all that mattered.

Moody was not the only preacher with such an interpretation, nor would he be the only one to accept corporate donations to preach a message of which the captains of industry approved. Decades later, as the United States shifted from the Second World War to the Cold War, Christian leaders capitalized on the "Red Panic" with the Spiritual Mobilization movement, inspired by the reactionary preaching of James W. Fifield Jr., who taught that both Christianity and capitalism "rested on a basic belief that individuals would succeed or fail on their own merit."[4] The message echoed Moody's emphasis on individual morality, and secured $125,000 from corporate donors in just a few months in 1948,[5] the equivalent of over $1.3 million in 2019 dollars.

Moody and Fifield are indicative of a much larger prosperity-driven interpretation of God that is fundamentally individualistic in nature and has been a contributing factor to the uneven record of organized labor from the nineteenth century to the twenty-first. Some Christian social conservatives once made common cause with progressive economics. William Jennings Bryan may be remembered for his adherence to Creationism and Prohibition, but he was also a staunch supporter of labor unions and workers' rights. But as the

---

3. Matthew Paul Turner, *Our Great Big American God: A Short History of Our Ever-Growing Deity* (Jericho Books, 2014), 130.

4. Kevin M. Kruse, *One Nation Under God: How Corporate America Invented Christian America* (Basic Books, 2015), 10.

5. Ibid., 22

individualistic, wealth-enabling theology of Moody and his successors became more deeply rooted in the American Christian vernacular, so has the decoupling of strong religiosity and strong commitment to workers' well-being.

The influence that Moody and his theological successors—who would often be similarly bankrolled by the wealthy classes—have had in ensuring that American Christianity is considerable. They moved predominantly white American Christianity even further away from upholding the economic needs of working and impoverished people, and for the direct benefit of the country's scions of wealth. Given the atmosphere of increasingly weaker and more weakly enforced labor laws in the twentieth and twenty-first centuries, it is not unfair to wonder how Moody's legacy may have impacted, for instance, the demise of labor unions. No matter how much Christians claim to the contrary, we are not immune to the winds of popular belief, and the emphasis on individualism at the expense of the common good has so thoroughly saturated the American zeitgeist that even pro-social-justice Christians can find themselves opposing the organized labor movement.

Related to this experience of seeing religious or social justice-oriented institutions not only fail to unionize but actively fight unionization is the phenomenon of religious belief not being enough to overcome cultural and institutional barriers to unionization. As we have seen throughout this chapter, despite the teachings of scripture, the history of Christianity does not always lend itself to doing right by the poor, the laborers, and the un- or under-employed.

While I was in seminary in the San Francisco Bay Area, a protracted labor struggle came to its unhappy end not far north of me in Santa Rosa, California. For six years, the Service Employees International Union (SEIU) and the Santa Rosa Memorial Hospital engaged in a drawn-out battle over the unionization of hospital employees.

Santa Rosa Memorial Hospital (SRMH) has its roots in the order of the Sisters of St. Joseph of Orange. Like many Roman Catholic hospitals, Santa Rosa Memorial represented a tradition of healthcare infused with social justice. Some of the Sisters of St. Joseph of Orange

had marched with Cesar Chavez's United Farm Workers in the 1960s
and '70s. Several of them were incarcerated for their activities on
behalf of striking farmworkers.[6]

After a great deal of vicious back-and-forth between workers,
management, and religious leadership, the campaign to unionize
Santa Rosa Memorial Hospital resulted in a failure of the workforce
to unionize. Intimidation by hospital management was part of their
successful antiunion campaign, made possible by "a weak and loosely
enforced labor law."[7]

The Santa Rosa case was somewhat unique as a labor organizing
action in that both workers and management/ownership claimed the
mantle of social justice, as opposed to the latter claiming the mantle
of, say, Christian paternalism, *noblesse oblige*, prosperity theology, or
some other syncretic blend of Christianity and pro-plutocratic sentiment in response to more pro-worker sentiment and action. However, it is precisely those syncretic blends that have contributed to the
creation of an economic climate in which organized labor has been
sacrificed on an altar of individualism and wealth-worship. While historical examples of individual Christian morality may seem on the surface to be unrelated to the erosion of workers' rights and livelihoods,
the line to be drawn between the two is both clear and relatively short.

Several decades before the SEIU/Santa Rosa Memorial struggle,
the Congress of Industrial Organizations (CIO) attempted to unionize the South. The Christian faith and culture of Southern workers
shaped their reactions to the large-scale unionization drive in the post-
World War II American South. The CIO's effort was named Operation Dixie, and it, like the SEIU attempt to unionize Santa Rosa
Memorial, ended ultimately in failure.

While there were institutional and statutory contributors to the
demise of Operation Dixie, such as the passage of the labor-union-
restricting Taft-Hartley Act in 1947 over President Harry Truman's
veto, there were more nuanced reasons for the campaign's failure.

---

6. Adam D. Reich, *With God on Our Side: The Struggle for Workers' Rights in a Catholic
Hospital* (Ithaca, NY: Cornell University Press, 2012), 2.

7. Ibid, 10.

Though individual Southerners often allied themselves with the CIO on the basis of their Christian values, those faith-based values were not enough to overcome the trust barriers of the regional culture and its suspicion of change. Union organizers were seen as carpetbaggers. The Red Scare of the late 1940s and 1950s added to the distrust of union organizers as suspected communists. White racism also diminished their chances of success. The religious and white supremacist parochialism of the United States that has shifted against workers' rights and protections remains a formidable economic and cultural force, in spite of the efforts of a number of Christian activists to the contrary.

Portraits of Faithful Activism

[E]vangelicalism has often resonated with the conviction enshrined in the old Wobblie hymn: There is power in a union.—Heath W. Carter[8]

For decades, clergy were heavily involved in campaigns concerning workers' wages and rights, including the right to organize. These clergy were informed by the very same prophetic biblical tradition, and the elevation of scripture is at the core of much of Christian labor activism: "Is the better question, 'Who was a neighbor to the [workers] and their families?' And then we might well hear a returning echo, 'Go, and do likewise'"[9] This definition of neighbor confounds the typically narrow definition of neighbor by way of geographic proximity, and it is vital to translating an understanding of this biblical parable into action.

To parish-based clergy, the unemployed, underemployed, and underpaid are our neighbors as well as our congregants, and how we treat them and minister to them must be in accord with Christ's own teachings. Generations of ministers have taken to the picket lines, preached sermons, written letters, and stood in solidarity with workers

---

8. Heath W. Carter, "The Church of Organized Labor," *The New Republic,* https://newrepublic.com/article/122279/church-organized-labor, July 12, 2015, accessed January 27, 2017.

9. Laurie Guy, "Prophetic or Pathetic? The Response of the Churches to the 1951 Waterfront Dispute," *Stimulus,* vol. 22, no. 2 (2015): 20.

who strove to both organize and better their financial security. Examples of this solidarity abound, even in a cursory survey of United States history. Some common denominators distinguish pro-labor and anti-racist activism from other forms of ministry and revolve around how ministers work to mediate the socioeconomic chasms between the wealthy and the workers that overlap with the chasm between whiteness and non-whiteness.

To better illustrate this pattern of activism and backlash, I offer two examples, both from the historically union-saturated terrain of Michigan. The first is that of the activist Presbyterian pastor Claude Williams and the organization of black and white auto workers in the 1940s and '50s. The second, more cautionary tale is that of Cardinal Adam Maida who tried to navigate the Detroit newspaper strikes of the mid-1990s.

Claude Williams, a radical Presbyterian evangelist and labor activist, was arrested multiple times during his ministry. Clergy are sometimes reflexively branded as communists or Marxists for involving themselves publicly in labor rights,[10] but the extent to which Williams was bordered on the extreme. He was framed by one opponent as part of a "MODERNISTIC, COMMUNISTIC ECCLESIASTICAL CONSPIRACY" (use of all caps in the original sources), "one of the rankest Communists in America," and a "Communist on the Presbyterian payroll."[11] During the Detroit race riots in the 1940s, he served as a chaplain to both white and black auto workers "to counter the antiblack preachings of some other [Detroit-area] religious leaders."[12] For Williams, who was committed to undoing both poverty and racism, the consequences of his commitment included not just the repeated verbal attacks; his presbytery eventually defrocked him as a heretic.[13]

---

10. Matthew Pehl, "'Apostles of Fascism,' 'Communist Clergy,' and the UAW: Political Ideology and Working-Class Religion in Detroit, 1919–1945." *Journal of American History.* vol. 99, no. 2 (2012): 464–65.

11. Ibid., 457.

12. Thomas A. Johnson, "Claude C. Williams: Organized Blacks," *The New York Times,* https://www.nytimes.com/1979/07/07/archives/claude-c-williams-organized-blacks-presbyterian-minister-84-worker.html, July 7, 1979, accessed August 26, 2019.

13. Ibid.

Identities of class and religious were interwoven in the prophetic tradition of ancient Israel. So, too, are they interwoven for clergy who ascribe to liberation theology, which expresses a preferential option for the poor and the working class. To side with the poor is not a prejudice to be dismantled, but is a biblical theology upon which to build. God's passion for the poor and oppressed is manifest across scripture, and those of us who hold those texts to be sacred cannot simultaneously see them as sacred and then dismiss their contents.

Direct lobbying by clergy and activists on behalf of the poor and the workers in their communities has produced a variety of results historically. It is often difficult to gauge their effectiveness, which can range from ordinances or statutes passed to enlisting the cultural cachet of local "elites" to advance the cause.[14] Religious sociologist William Mirola looks at the actions of Cardinal Adam Maida in Detroit, who tried to balance the demands of the striking newspaper workers who asked for his support during their strike of 1995 to 1997 with the access to the newspaper's management and local politicians that his position afforded him.

> As Archbishop of an entire religious community that included both strikers and management, Cardinal Maida had to negotiate two competing sets of interests in Detroit. Morally, he had to condemn the use of replacement workers but without completely alienating the newspaper's management on whom he would depend to address future community issues.[15]

Maida's dilemma of neutrality illustrates that we cannot measure the effectiveness of clergy with only one yardstick. Maida had hoped to persuade community leaders on a number of issues, so he did not want to alienate them on this particular one. He was not able to bring about any of the change the newspaper workers demanded. Individual

---

14. William Mirola, "Religious Protest and Economic Conflict: Possibilities and Constraints on Religious Resource Mobilization and Coalitions in Detroit's Newspaper Strike." *Sociology of Religion*. vol. 64, no. 4. (2003): 453.

15. Ibid.

Catholics in Detroit supported the striking workers, but under Maida, the archdiocese itself did not.

Parishioners who belong to a labor union and their pastors may live alongside each other, yet the differences between them can hinder effective coalition-building.[16] The "cultures of competition" between different demographics within a community can lead to strategic differences, and create a chasm between clergy and union workers.[17] The tendency of clergy to deemphasize labor and economic concerns in favor of individual morality fits neatly in the arc of preachers like Dwight Moody and James Fifield Jr. Ultimately, the laity tend to be more supportive of labor unions than clergy.

While Cardinal Maida may be a cautionary tale, the American history of activism on behalf of the working poor owes a great debt to the Roman Catholic tradition, as far back as Pope Leo XIII's pivotal encyclical *Rerum Novarum,* which couched the issues of fair pay and the right to organize in the Christian language of justice and equality. Leo XIII's social teaching has been lived out by generations of Roman Catholic labor activists and clergy across the United States.

Roman Catholic activism on behalf of the poor and blue-collar workers should be considered by faith communities today not as some long-ago abstract phenomenon but as the fundamental work of the Gospel. By affording it the same deference the church affords traditions of worship, preaching, and other spiritual practices, congregations can then take the step of asking how they can live out such solidarity with the workers in their own communities.

Finally, a word ought to be spoken on the value of learning from the history of both the church and organized labor. The history of the church is fraught with violence on both personal and systemic levels, and many labor unions have an uncomfortable history of racism that has yet to be truly reckoned with. The need to understand and interpret these histories in a way that serves the causes of racial justice and wage justice is urgent. Whilst recognizing the example previous clergy and labor leaders of faith have set for contemporary clergy has merit,

16. Ibid., 457.
17. Ibid.

so too does acknowledging that history cannot, and should not, simply be repeated or replicated for history's sake. Rather, these histories must be learned from and reflected upon, lest the sins of prior generations be committed anew. Indeed, learning from the (often grievous) sins of our predecessors not only has merit, but is an immediate ethical imperative if one is to indeed better the chances of social justice, including economic justice.

Because of this, we cannot simply pretend that this racist aspect of the history of organized labor in the United States does not exist. To do so would be a disservice, especially to those who have historically been excluded from labor organizing on account of their race, ethnicity, nationality, or sexual orientation or identity.

The historical exclusivity and hierarchy of many labor unions has not served those unions, or the workers they lay claim to representing, well. How we both make history and reflect on it are of great importance as we study strikes, work stoppages, and other labor actions. The historical exclusivity and hierarchy of many labor unions has not served the workers they claim to represent well. Similarly, whom the labor movement chooses to include or exclude sets up future precedents for inclusion and exclusion, and those precedents have often historically been deployed at the behest of prejudices rather than the economic and social advancement of workers.

A Snapshot in Time: Cowlitz County, Washington[18]

During the late summer and early autumn of 2015, two labor strikes shook Cowlitz County, Washington, where I ministered for nearly seven years. Longview, Washington, and its neighbor, Kelso, were built around the timber, pulp, and papermaking industries. The pulp and paper mills were the largest employers in the area. The Kelso and Longview public school districts were not far behind. In just a few weeks, both the millworkers at the largest mill and the

---

18. Unless otherwise noted, all source material for this section is derived from my doctoral thesis for Seattle University's School of Theology and Ministry: *For More Than Ashes: A Qualitative Study on the Role of Christian Values in Labor Organizing in Cowlitz County, Washington* (ProQuest, 2018).

teachers in Kelso went on strike for both economic and workplace safety reasons. The Association of Western Pulp and Paper Workers (AWPPW) Local 153 and the Kelso Education Association (KEA) both engaged in extensive organizing and communication efforts to both execute the strikes and explain their necessity to the wider community.

The membership of AWPPW #153 had been cut in half over the four decades since its last strike. The members had worked for a year and a half without a collective bargaining agreement after the previous one had expired.[19] The KEA strike in Kelso was part of a wave of teacher strikes across Washington State in protest of the meager resources provided by a state legislature so dysfunctional that, in 2012, it was held in contempt by the state supreme court for refusing to pass a budget that adequately funded public schools; they were eventually fined $100,000 a day as a result.[20]

Both strikes profoundly affected the people of Cowlitz County. Employees of some of the largest area employers now had to subsist on strike pay, picket lines became part of the normal scenery, and nastiness spilled over into the public dialogue, like the anonymous letter I received. While many people tangibly supported the striking workers, it was a stressful and tumultuous time for the workers. They became the subject of my doctoral thesis. I wanted to know what the strikers, the community, the clergy, and the church people thought the role of the church should be in the middle of a labor action. I asked them about their memories of the strikes, what role the strikes played in their lives and livelihoods, and whether they felt that churches and clergy have a role

19. Marissa Luck, "AWPPW Accepts Contract," *The Daily News,* http://tdn.com/news/local/awppw-accepts-contract/article_839e38ae-9b97-5614-a01b-9809e4e166bc.html, December 14, 2016, accessed April 4, 2018.

20. Melissa Santos, "High Court Orders $100,000-per-Day Fine to Continue in McCleary School Funding Case," *The News Tribune,* https://www.thenewstribune.com/news/politics-government/article106406507.html, October 6, 2016, accessed March 2, 2019. This statewide concern remained even after the KEA strike ended. In 2018, three years after the KEA strike, the public school teachers in Longview similarly went on strike as part of another statewide wave of labor actions by teachers in protest of the meager pay and resources they were afforded by the state.

to play when labor actions occur. I asked them to react to one another's responses, to rate how strongly they felt about their own responses, and to rate the importance of differing points of view they heard throughout the process. In their answers, I saw what common themes of agreement or disagreement existed, and what areas of consensus a local church might be able to build around in determining how it might respond to labor actions in the future.

The results I discovered were, in many cases, marked in their near-unanimity. The people I interviewed were theologically and denominationally diverse: Roman Catholic, Protestant, and nonde-nominational Christians. Yet almost everyone saw a need and had a desire for local congregations to address labor concerns in their communities, suggesting an appetite for not simply reactive, but proactive, ministry from congregations and clergy. Almost everyone said the church should offer a safe place for conversations around issues of labor and organizing. They also said the church should help parishioners discern how best to respond as Christians to strikes or labor actions.

Their consensus is the biggest reason you are holding this book in your hands: people want the church to be active in tackling points of contention, facilitating constructive discussions, and spiritually preparing people. However, most of the Bible studies and faith formation tools I have seen in my decade of parish ministry offer little of the sort to the church. The data tells me that there is a definite need, and we should be paying attention to—and trying to meet—that need.

Finally, this series of surveys has the potential to act as a tool in your own context. This process was designed in part to be relatively easily replicable across an array of congregational ministry contexts and denominations/faith traditions. If you want to discover how the clergy in your area, or members of a union local in your town, feel about religious involvement in workers' rights and labor organizing, there is nothing stopping you—and this is one way to go about it! It was an honor for me to hear directly from

the people doing the hard work not only of their jobs, but of organizing themselves and their coworkers to further each other's livelihoods and rights. That work is divine in nature, and to document
some small part of it was a blessing.

Conversations of what to do, and how to go about doing it, will
be mighty and likely difficult, but their urgency still stands before
us, demanding to be addressed. That an anonymous troll saw fit to
detract from that work in my mail one day is just one illustration
of the fierce imperative to dismantle the dehumanizing mentality
of the present in favor of a future that affirms the worth of a person and their labor.

If you are able to hear from lower-wage workers and poor—
and perhaps count yourself among them—in your context, there
are important ways in which the presence of faith-based allies can
help. Specifically, introducing the language of morality is a vital
aspect of this work that is fundamentally economic, but cannot be
framed only in economics. My college friend Scott Cheesewright
is a Portland, Oregon-based labor union organizer. We were on
the speech and debate team together at Lewis & Clark College.
We spent many long weekends at tournaments across the country; now he uses the critical thinking skills he honed during those
weekends to work on behalf of justice for workers, which includes
allying with faith communities. He says, "Managers will talk with
people of faith. People taken as a respected other party that can,
if you will, show management the light. Bosses will dig in beyond
the point that it makes sense as a show of their power because
unionization represents a real loss to them. The introduction of
faithful and moral language can help break them out of that."[21]

Nor does the impact of faith language have to be limited to inter-
actions with managers. "Labor organizing can be polarizing, but when
faith leaders say that working conditions or low wages are wrong, they

---

21. Scott Cheesewright, transcribed personal interview, Portland, Oregon, August 29, 2019.

can be heard—by outsiders and by other workers—in a way that the organizing workers may not be heard."[22]

Using faith language to amplify workers' voices not only to people of power, but also to other workers, can be done in more than one way. The Poor People's Campaign, inspired by Martin Luther King Jr.'s eponymous 1968 campaign and led by Disciples of Christ pastor William J. Barber II and Presbyterian pastor Liz Theoharis, works with local organizing bodies across the country to create visibility for economic concerns that are simultaneously local and nationwide. It represents one way of utilizing faith to frame the needs of poor and working people as a right rather than an entitlement. Cheesewright underlines why this is so important:

> Management may try to frame worker demands as unreasonable or wrong, and support of faith leaders can offer a strength of conviction for what workers are organizing for. When workers organize, they're in a position where their livelihoods, and those of their families and communities, are put at risk. You naturally start asking, "Am I doing the right thing?" Faith leaders can provide strength for those convictions in a way that simple economics cannot.[23]

Honoring all of God's people is a basic part of labor organizing and advocacy; the church cannot forget this fundamental truth. We are all a part of this history of the divine economy. How we shape our small part of this history depends on how well we are equipped. Though labor actions speak to our most basic needs—to earn a livelihood, to attain some semblance of financial security, and to work with a sense of dignity—the church has not always equipped the faithful to respond to those needs in a way that reflects the teachings of Jesus Christ. The church has responded with pockets of justice, but too often, we have abdicated our moral authority where it might have done good, or in electing to actively inflict harm.

---

22. Ibid.
23. Ibid.

. Being honest about our history teaches us to defer to the narratives of those who have been harmed, repair credibility and relationships both inside and outside the church, learn from our past to help shape our future, and, most of all, uphold the innate value taught by Jesus that the truth can set us free.

CHAPTER 6

The Dispossession of Children and Elders
Wealth and Generational Status

I have a master's degree in my field. Because I juggled five different scholarships and had a supportive family, the degree did not add to my debt. I know I am one of the lucky ones.

I just got a new job after being unemployed for several months, in which time I depleted my savings and maxed out my MasterCard. I am currently living paycheck to paycheck as I work to pay off my credit card debt and car loan. I now pay more in income taxes than ExxonMobil, Chevron, Boeing, and Bank of America combined paid in 2009 . . .

I am the 99 percent.[1]

I wrote those words the autumn of 2011, just after I began my first full-time pastorate in Longview, Washington. I posted it anonymously on the website *We Are the 99 Percent*, which gave the Occupy Wall Street movement its motto.

I chose my words for that post carefully, not wanting to cast aspersions on my new employer. I was offered fair compensation in a vocation where no one should expect to get rich. But even with financial aid from my alma mater, my denomination, and multiple outside scholarships helping to pay for my master's of divinity, and with my

---

1. Eric Atcheson, untitled, http://wearethe99percent.tumblr.com/post/10796371815/i-have-a-masters-degree-in-my-field-because-i, September 29, 2011, accessed September 10, 2018.

family behind me, I was still one of the rising millennial graduates to begin their careers in debt.

This awareness of the debt our generation was taking on was present even at the start of the Great Recession in 2008. As I, several of my classmates at Lewis & Clark College, and our chaplain were planning a special commencement weekend worship service, a running gag in our planning sessions was to theme the service after the verse in the Lord's Prayer, "forgive us our debts."

Joking aside, the consequences my generation faces as a result of its economic predicament are dire. Financial precariousness can go hand-in-hand with health precariousness, and millennials are now dying at "alarming" rates as a result of suicide, drug overdoses, and more.[2] Far from being a subject for punchlines, the current economy is a matter of life-and-death for young adults.

Millennials are not the only ones to suffer the financial consequences of the Great Recession. Many small neighborhood churches routinely run annual deficits, relying on savings or more debt in order to keep their doors open. I have seen a number of congregations, both inside and outside my denomination, close. While those closures were usually done with purpose, they still serve as reminders to a young pastor of the precariousness of a church's existence. My hope is that the church will recognize that precariousness in the lives of its younger generations and meet it with empathy that is born of experience.

However, the discussion of generational poverty need not, and should not, be limited to my own millennial generation and Generation Z behind us. Our elders are facing disproportionate challenges of destroyed savings and personal bankruptcies right as they should be riding off into the sunset of well-deserved retirements. And so, this chapter will end with consideration of the unique dilemmas our elders face, and of what the church might do to be salt and light for our seniors.

---

2. Joel Achenbach, "'There's Something Terribly Wrong': Americans Are Dying Young at Alarming Rates," Washington Post, https://www.washingtonpost.com/health/theres-something-terribly-wrong-americans-are-dying-young-at-alarming-rates/2019/11/25/d88b28ec-0d6a-11ea-8397-a955cd542d00_story.html, November 25, 2019, accessed December 12, 2019.

The Student Debt Crisis

While the Occupy movement made many of its headlines in 2011 with its presence at Zuccotti Park in New York City, it was a series of actions it took in 2013–14 that caught my attention anew, thanks to its obvious biblical connotations: the Rolling Jubilee. Named for the Year of Jubilee found in Leviticus 25—a passage we discussed at length in chapter 2—Occupy's Rolling Jubilee was meant to hearken back to the forgiveness not just of spiritual sins, but of tangible financial debts.

The Rolling Jubilee began in 2013 with an outlay of four hundred thousand dollars to buy out—and subsequently forgive—nearly fifteen million dollars' worth of medical debt owed by more than two thousand people.[3] Occupy followed up the 2013 Jubilee with a 2014 Jubilee that forgave nearly four million dollars' worth of student loan debt owed to for-profit institutions, with Occupy buying out the debt for approximately three cents on the dollar.[4]

As of the summer of 2018, outstanding student debt totaled over one-and-a-half trillion dollars.[5] Even when adjusted for inflation, the price of both private and public education has skyrocketed over the past few decades. While many schools have increased their commitment to financial aid, the rising costs have largely been passed on to students and their families in tuition hikes and additional fees.

To cover the prohibitive price tag of a college education, millennials took out federally backed student loans. For many of us, paying off these loans feels like a treadmill from hell. What little we can afford to pay in a low-wage economy goes to interest, and the principal of the loan remains unchanged. Though it is not the sort of debt slavery condemned by the Hebrew prophets, economic exploitation is not an unfair term to apply to student loans.

---

3. Vauhini Vara, "The Occupy Movement Takes On Student Debt," *The New Yorker,* https://www.newyorker.com/business/currency/occupy-movement-takes-student-debt, September 17, 2014, accessed September 13, 2018.

4. Ibid.

5. The $1.5 trillion figure of outstanding student loan debt does not include private loans not backed by the federal government, the total of which is, according to many estimates, likely in excess of $100 billion.

The debt crisis, along with other bleak financial realities for millennials, has created a sad irony for our participation in most any kind of Christian faith community. We are wanted for our youth, vitality, and young children, but the enthusiastic welcome for our presence can morph into resentment when congregants realize that we cannot afford to tithe or significantly pledge to our churches. The myth of the young family with money is precisely that—a myth—and young families can end up quietly resented in the pews for not living up to that myth.

As more baby boomer pastors begin to retire, the ranks of the clergy will be made up of millennials and Generation X. Many of those pastors will still have significant student debt. Congregations that may not be accustomed to compensating their clergy with a sufficient enough salary to cover seminary loan repayments need strategize on how they can best afford to fairly pay their seminary-educated clergy, whether for the sake of their current staff or for the next pastor they call.

Congregations—and even regional, conference, or diocesan ministries—should consider establishing a small scholarship fund for its college students. I am under no illusions about the coffers of most churches, but this is not about creating an additional budget burden; it is about making a gesture of solidarity with overstretched students. The scholarship does not have to be big. A few hundred dollars can pay for a student's used textbooks. The money maintains a tangible connection between the student and their home church, and the savings add up to much more once the years of interest on additional loans are taken into account.

On a structural level, churches can research how colleges, universities, and seminaries affiliated with their denominations can help to mitigate the student debt crisis. Does the denomination have investments that contribute to student debt (such as stock in for-profit education companies)? Can they divest? Do schools affiliated with your denomination hold such assets in their endowments, and can those assets be feasibly divested? What are the potential fundraising avenues for new scholarships?

One of the most effective measures my denomination has taken in the past five years has been to make the master's of divinity degree tuition-free for its students at a few partner seminaries on the West Coast. Textbooks and the exorbitant cost of living still remain financial obstacles to Disciples of Christ seminarians on the West Coast, but tuition no longer does. As Christians add our voices to the larger political sphere in favor of equitable economic policies, our congregations and denominations can make small moves as well.

Some of our political leaders appear more willing to tackle the student debt crisis in radical ways. During the opening stages of the Democratic presidential process, Massachusetts senator Elizabeth Warren proposed a policy that would forgive the majority of currently held student debt, make public colleges tuition-free, and set aside specific funds for historically black colleges and universities (HBCUs).[6] Philanthropist Robert Smith, an African American, used his commencement address at Morehouse College, an HBCU, to tell them he was paying off the entire debt of the graduating class—an estimated $40 million.[7] The latter represents the drastic need for the former.

The student debt crisis is not only a generational crisis, but a gendered crisis as well. When women are financially punished for both choosing and not choosing to have children, the acuity of their punishment is exacerbated by the debt incurred by their education, creating unsustainable and immoral financial demands on half the populace.

Parental Leave

Carrie and I had a couple of baby showers for our first child. One was with our close friends in the Portland area, a highly informal

---

6. Janet Watson, "History Lesson: Sen. Elizabeth Warren Breaks Down Why Her $50 Billion Plan to Fund HBCUs Is Very Necessary," *The Root,* https://www.theroot.com/history-lesson-sen-elizabeth-warren-breaks-down-why-h-1834445016, May 1, 2019, accessed June 20, 2019.

7. Bo Emerson, "Morehouse Commencement Speaker to Pay Off Class of 2019's Student Loans," *The Atlanta Journal-Constitution,* https://www.ajc.com/news/just-morehouse-commencement-speaker-pay-off-class-2019-student-loans/XvMHlS1SVyJiG3mRp1WOWL/, May 19, 2019, accessed June 20, 2019.

affair. The other was across the country at her parents' church in North Carolina, where I got to experience an old-fashioned church baby shower in a parlor, replete with Baptist punch and ham biscuits.

Before the shower, we attended worship with Carrie's parents and an interesting thing happened. My expectations for the sermon were not just met; they were exceeded. The pastor delivered a message on the commandment to honor the Sabbath. Beyond our personal need for rest, he talked about the communal dimensions of the Sabbath. Sometimes, he said, we need to give others a rest from us. The Sabbath is one of the mandates in the Torah that demand justice from God's people. To honor the Sabbath meant not just days off and vacations, but also parental leave. He called out companies that fired women for asking for maternity leave. A culture that devalued family leave did not honor the Sabbath. My pregnant wife and I had scrimped and saved for months so she could take a proper—yet unpaid—maternity leave when our child arrived, and I nearly stood up and shouted, "Amen!"

Many factors have contributed to our collective devaluing of parental leave, but, as people of faith, we should see the devaluing as an unjust affront to the biblical command to keep the Sabbath. Yet what we have replaced the Sabbath tradition with is what the German sociologist Max Weber termed the "Protestant work ethic" in his landmark work *The Protestant Ethic and the Spirit of Capitalism*. And while Weber coined this term on the basis of his work in Europe, it has been the United States that has embraced a culture of workaholism as a central part of our civic religion of Christianity.

Access to paid parental leave in the United States is scattershot at best. Only 13 percent of workers in private industry receive paid family leave. In industries like construction and hospitality, only 5–6 percent.[8] While access to unpaid family leave is common, thanks to the Family and Medical Leave Act of 1993, the paucity of paid

---

8. Drew DeSilver, "Access to Paid Family Leave Varies Widely across Employers, Industries," Pew Research Center, http://www.pewresearch.org/fact-tank/2017/03/23/access-to-paid-family-leave-varies-widely-across-employers-industries/, March 23, 2017, accessed August 31, 2018.

parental leave marks the United States as an outlier among industrialized nations.

Combined with the reality of crippling student loan debt, young people are between a rock and a hard place. Millennial parents may be tempted to take parental leave as late as possible or return to work as soon as possible due to financial reasons. While this dilemma affects all parents regardless of gender, it financially punishes women in particular. After she returns to work, a mother may need time off to pump breast milk or attend to postpartum health concerns, which leaves her vulnerable to an unsympathetic employer.

More millennials are postponing parenthood, or choosing to not become parents at all. In 2016, 48 percent of female millennials were mothers; by this point in Generation X's timeline, 57 percent of females had become mothers.[9] When asked, millennials place the same importance on parenthood as our generational predecessors,[10] which suggests it is not that millennials do not want to be parents, but that we do not think the time is right.

It is not that millennials do not take parenthood seriously. Rather, I think we grasp the gravity of it and are waiting for the best moment to assume that soul-sized responsibility. Churches that are eager for us to immediately begin families because that has been the way for generations need to listen to our perspective. Delays in child-bearing are not a sign of millennial immaturity, but maturity, and of the seriousness with which we take parenthood's demands.

Contraception and Daycare

For me, as a male pastor, to weigh in on the issue of contraception is particularly fraught. Many women have been scolded and shamed by male pastors over contraception as part of a patriarchal paradigm for which the church must repent.

---

9. Gretchen Livingston, "More Than a Million Millennials Are Becoming Moms Each Year," Pew Research Center, http://www.pewresearch.org/fact-tank/2018/05/04/more-than-a-million-millennials-are-becoming-moms-each-year/, May 4, 2018, accessed September 6, 2018.

10. Ibid.

I believe that contraception should be universally affordable and accessible—not just for reasons of civil liberty and human autonomy, but as a matter economic justice.

Out-of-pocket spending on oral contraception has plummeted since it came under the Affordable Care Act. Hormonal birth control is not solely an elective course of medication for preventing pregnancy. It gets prescribed for medical conditions like endometriosis, and access to it is finally being treated as the public health need that it has always been. The percentage of women paying out-of-pocket for oral contraception dropped from roughly 21 percent in 2012—when the ACA provision came into effect—to just over 6 percent in 2013, and to 3 percent in 2015.[11] And the average estimated savings per woman on hormonal birth control, whether in the form of the pill or an intrauterine device (IUD), has been approximately $250 per year.[12] Especially when the gendered wage gap remains real, accessible contraception remains a moral and financial imperative.

Christian opposition to funding contraception must be weighed against the repeated commands in the New Testament to safeguard the basic financial security of others. Access to contraception as a vital subset to access to healthcare should be interpreted through the lens of Jesus healing the women who came to him. I do not doubt the sincerity of those who do not want to cover contraception in their healthcare plans for religious reasons, but think their religious reasons disregard all of those healing stories and teachings on financial security from the Gospels.

To tend to the health of the person is to tend to the health of their particular sex or gender. For men, that includes treatment for prostate and testicular cancers—for which awareness campaigns are never controversial. For women, it should include hormonal contraception, whether for elective or medically necessitated purposes. The healthcare for everyone needs to include comprehensive sex education in

---

11. Sam Petulla, "3 Ways Obamacare Changed Birth Control," CNN, https://www
.cnn.com/2017/10/07/politics/obamacare-changed-birth-control-contraceptives/index.html,
October 7, 2017, accessed October 3, 2018.

12. Ibid.

the classroom, including on the topic of consent. The stakes are too high for Christians to keep pretending that abstinence-only education works. It is the aspartame of health classes for our children: artificial in its origins, cloying in its delivery, and unhealthy in its effects. Healthier ways to teach sex education must be embraced by the church because of our own ethical and theological commitments to human flourishing.

Just as the prevention of childbirth must be discussed as healthcare from an economic justice perspective, so too must childrearing itself. For families with children, the cost of childcare is akin to a second rent or mortgage check, and constitutes one of the most expensive items in their monthly budget.

The Department of Health and Human Services considers childcare to be "affordable" if its cost does not exceed 7 percent of the median household income for a married couple.[13] However, only one state—Louisiana—meets that standard.[14] For single parents, the relative cost of childcare is almost certainly even more prohibitive.

The average monthly cost of daycare here in Washington State would have been the most expensive line item in our household budget—more than our mortgage, more than our student loan payments, more than anything. Carrie and I quickly realized that it was more economically viable, and more emotionally satisfying, to have our parents act as our primary daycare once we both returned to work, even though it meant renting an apartment for her parents and reserving the occasional extended stay hotel room for mine.

On the one hand, our setup is family at its best: grandparents from literally across the nation pitching in to help raise their first grandchild. On the other hand, parents should not need their own parents to drop everything and offer childcare, nor is that even an option for a great many parents. Accessible, affordable childcare should not be dependent on having family close by or a certain level of wealth in

---

13. Grover J. "Russ" Whitehurst, "Why the Federal Government Should Subsidize Childcare and How to Pay for It," The Brookings Institution, https://www.brookings.edu/research/why-the-federal-government-should-subsidize-childcare-and-how-to-pay-for-it/, March 9, 2017, accessed September 30, 2018.

14. Ibid.

order to afford daycare. But that is the system we have created, and it is a system the church should aim to fix.

Many congregations operate schools, preschools, or daycare centers; others rent portions of their space to independent daycare or preschools. In my career, I have served parishes that have done both. For congregations that operate their own, how do your tuition rates and enrollment policies (if any) create a student body that is or is not necessarily reflective of your neighborhood? Does your faculty and staff reflect your neighborhood? Do you represent a financially realistic option to families, especially families of color, in your area?

These questions about whether or not you reflect your surrounding neighborhood are also good questions for your spiritual community at large—congregations can be sources of babysitters and childcare pinch-hitters for parents, and many parents evaluate congregations when "church shopping" in no small part based on the congregation's Sunday school, children's church, and other children's ministries. This reality should highlight to churches the importance of quality children's ministries, and to parents the importance of community in raising our children. That community, in turn, should reflect the diverse world our children will one day be entrusted with stewarding as we have.

The increased demand for well-qualified childcare is not an indicator of the decline of the traditional family unit in the United States. The real value of wages for most Americans has not kept pace with the demand for daycare, which is ironic because the demand is largely propelled by how many hours parents have to work. In other words, parents are not being paid enough to provide for our children.

The Gig Economy

A variety of economic factors—student loan debt, parental leave, access to contraception and daycare—are falling heaviest upon millennials at present (and Generation Z is up next). The movement away from the employer-employee model of labor to an independent contractor-client economy has had a profoundly negative impact on employer-provided benefits like a pension and health insurance, as well as on the ability of a workforce to organize.

The gig economy, in which increasing numbers of jobs are made available only on a temporary or independent contractor basis as opposed to a permanent or employer-employee basis, represents a paradigm of employment that has left my generation underemployed and likely with permanently stunted lifetime earning potentials. As I documented in *Oregon Trail Theology*, millennials earn, on average, 20 percent less than baby boomers did at the same point in their lives. Millennial workers have an average net worth of $8,000, which represents a 34-percent drop since 1996.[15] They are not only earning less than their predecessors, but are not getting the same sort of benefits as our predecessors, like traditional pensions. And in the gig economy, they are finding it harder to find full-time work.

When the oldest millennials entered the workforce, traditional pensions were already becoming a thing of the past—the simple fact that I am a millennial with a pension plan (through the Disciples Pension Fund) makes me the exception, not the rule. Only 23 percent of all workers in the United States currently participate in a pension plan, and for workers in the private sector, that number drops to just 15 percent.[16]

But even the 401(k) retirement plans that replaced the traditional 403(b) pensions are often not available or accessible to workers, especially to those who are minimum wage workers or are treated as independent contractors rather than as employees, as suggested by the reality that nearly half of all workers in the United States—46 percent—do not participate any sort of workplace retirement plan.[17] Meanwhile, the Affordable Care Act was necessitated in no small part

---

15. Abha Bhattarai, "The Average Millennial Has an Average Net Worth of $8,000. That's Far Less Than Previous Generations," *The Washington Post*, https://www.washingtonpost.com/business/2019/05/31/millennials-have-an-average-net-worth-thats-significantly-less-than-previous-generations/?utm_term=.b0a87ca49e09, May 31, 2019, accessed June 1, 2019.

16. "How Many American Workers Participate in Workplace Retirement Plans?" Pension Rights Center, http://www.pensionrights.org/publications/statistic/how-many-american-workers-participate-workplace-retirement-plans, January 18, 2018, accessed October 9, 2018.

17. Ibid.

because another aspect of the more traditional employer-employee relationship—employer-provided health insurance—was out of the reach of tens of millions of Americans in no small part because of both unemployment and underemployment.

The monthly federal report on jobs and unemployment is a surface-level snapshot of the economy. What is not presented in media reports is the gauging of underemployment: people who want full-time work, but can only find part-time, seasonal, or independent contractor positions, all of which, generally, offer few benefits. This is the gig economy.

Only recently have statistics documenting the genuine struggle that gig economy workers face become widely available. In California, the largest state economy in the United States and one of the largest world economies in its own right, roughly one in ten people work in the gig economy. Nearly half of them struggle with poverty.[18] Five percent of the population lives on the verge of poverty even though they are technically "employed." What is seen as a full recovery from the Great Recession statistically has only been so for the wealthiest among us. The recovery is partial at best for the rest of us. We live in an age of wage stagnation, reductions in union membership, and the decline in employer-provided health and retirement benefits.

Finally, the difficulty of organizing workers into labor union locals—a process that faces a long series of obstacles already when the workers are classified as employees—is all but insurmountable with workers who are independent contractors. And the companies that employ these workers very much want to keep matters this way. However, gig economy workers in some industries, such as ridesharing, are beginning to organize themselves for better pay and benefits.

In May 2019, drivers around the world for the ridesharing companies Uber and Lyft went on a daylong strike to draw attention to how the two corporations had purposefully scaled back wages over the

---

18. Alex Vandermaas-Peeler et al, "A Renewed Struggle for the American Dream: PRRI 2018 California Workers Survey," *PRRI*, https://www.prri.org/research/renewed_struggle_for_the_american_dream-prri_2018_california_workers_survey/#, August 28, 2018, accessed May 31, 2019.

years. Uber drivers, who are paid per mile, saw their per-mile wage rates slashed by 25 percent by the company,[19] forcing drivers to work longer hours to make the same money.[20]

Other driving service companies that rely on independent contractors expect their workers to dedicate a certain number of hours if they want the best schedules or opportunities for tips. Instacart, a food delivery app, requires workers to dedicate at least ninety hours over three weeks—an average of thirty hours per week—for the privilege of predictable hours[21] that would be a matter of course in many more traditional employment settings. For many, the gig economy has become a financially losing proposition.

Think of how the Hebrew prophets insisted on prompt payment of a laborer's wage. Think of how James condemned the denial of fairly earned wages to the hired hand. Those verses offer a theological disapproval of the gig economy that avoids paying workers fairly and promptly, and abdicates responsibility for healthcare and retirement. Too often, the church has stood by and allowed, or even encouraged, employers to take advantage of their workers. The church must act as both a prophetic and dialogic agent to speak truth in the public square and to facilitate discussion about how to improve the financial security of the underemployed. We cannot allow this to become another abdicated responsibility.

Economic Justice and Climate Change

In the late summer of 2019, a sixteen-year-old Swedish teenager took the world by storm. Sailing across the Atlantic Ocean via boat

---

19. Luz Lazo, "Strike by Uber and Lyft Drivers Has Potential to Disrupt Travel for Thousands," *The Washington Post,* https://www.washingtonpost.com/transportation/2019/05/07/strike-by-uber-lyft-drivers-wednesday-has-potential-disrupt-travel-thousands/?utm_term=.4db746f19886, May 7, 2019, accessed May 8, 2019.

20. In any discussions of pay for rideshare drivers, it should be noted that they are typically responsible for all of the expenses related to operating their vehicle, from gas and maintenance to insurance and depreciation, all of which eat substantially into their effective net income.

21. Alina Selyukh, "Why Suburban Moms are Delivering Your Groceries," *National Public Radio,* https://www.npr.org/2019/05/25/722811953/why-suburban-moms-are-delivering-your-groceries, May 25, 2019, accessed May 31, 2019.

in order to minimize the carbon emissions of her journey, Greta Thunberg arrived in the United States and organized global strikes, addressed the United Nations, and united with other Generation Z activists around the world to take legal action against the environmental effects of climate change. And now, she is *Time* magazine's person of the year for 2019.

Climate change represents an existential threat to younger generations as a result of global warming from the actions of older generations. It is human-caused, scientifically demonstrated, and ignored or minimized completely at our own peril. Yet it has been ignored and minimized by successive decades of political leaders, and communities of faith are capable of responding to this dereliction by reframing climate change as a religious and economic justice concern in addition to a scientific one.

The economic damage wrought by natural disasters that are increasing in strength as climate change sets in is relatively quantifiable. In 2017, Hurricane Harvey inflicted an estimated $125 billion in damage to the Houston area, while Hurricane Sandy did roughly $71 billion in damage to the New York area in 2012.[22] This is on top of the unquantifiable human cost of such natural disasters, for as events such as the 2010 Haiti earthquake demonstrated, the loss of human life is often far higher in impoverished areas that have not benefited from the same level of construction and development as industrialized areas.

The strengthening of natural disasters via climate change represents an economic justice concern by itself: poorer areas are far more likely to be impacted the hardest, and the economic damage done by natural disasters is increasingly stratospheric. Additionally, the economic damage that areas from agriculture to infrastructure are facing down as a result of climate change are similarly staggering, to the tune of trillions of dollars.[23] These are areas of society that humanity relies

---

22. Renee Cho, "How Climate Change Impacts the Economy," *State of the Planet*, Columbia University, https://blogs.ei.columbia.edu/2019/06/20/climate-change-economy-impacts/ June 20, 2019, accessed September 26, 2019.

23. Ibid.

upon for both life and livelihood, and if our experience with natural disasters is any indication, impoverished areas are going to feel these consequences the most acutely.

But there is also a generational component to climate change as a matter of economic justice. Because of the basic reality of average human lifespans, millennials and Generation Z are likely to be the generations tasked with coping with, and responding to, the worst effects of climate change that are still yet to come. Greta Thunberg has long since acknowledged the reality that it is younger generations who will involuntarily bear this burden, and she is dedicating her life to ensuring that we recognize it as well. Coping with the effects of climate change will necessitate great economic cost at a minimum, potentially great human cost, and already a great environmental cost as many scientists are already arguing that the earth has entered its first mass-extinction-level event since the extinction of the dinosaurs.[24]

In the face of such dire consequences, it is increasingly vital for faith communities to respond to climate change in public and substantive ways. Organizing participation in a local climate strike, as hundreds of thousands of people have now done, is one way congregations can work to effect change. In my Disciples of Christ denomination, congregations can pursue Green Chalice status, which certifies that a congregation has engaged in an energy audit and made a series of changes to its consumption that substantially reduce its use of nonrenewable resources, and has taken steps to engage their wider communities on environmental concerns. Congregations in denominations without such a program can lobby to create one, or go about the steps of auditing and reducing their energy consumption on their own.

Faith communities must also take seriously the twin mandates to faithfully steward both the earth and our children as gifts created by God. Their futures are intertwined with our present: how we act in

---

24. Damian Carrington, "Earth's Sixth Mass Extinction Event Under Way, Scientists Warn," *The Guardian,* https://www.theguardian.com/environment/2017/jul/10/earths-sixth-mass-extinction-event-already-underway-scientists-warn, July 10, 2017, accessed September 26, 2019.

the present moment is an expression of whether or how we value their futures. If the church is going to be a body that cherishes future incarnations of itself, and of God's creation, then faithful public witness on our part urgently needs to be an integral part of our spirituality.

Retiring into Bankruptcy

As the social safety nets of Social Security and Medicare continue their long, slow fall into insolvency, the finances of many recent retirees have experienced a much sharper shock. As professor and labor expert Erik Loomis of the University of Rhode Island says, "The idea of retiring seems impossible even for many baby boomers, who have significant consumer debt and shaky finances as they reach their later years."[25]

The average sum saved for retirement currently tops out at $71,000. Personal bankruptcies among retirees have increased fivefold since 1991.[26] Just as with millennials and our legendary affinity for avocado toast, we cannot simply point our fingers at individual spending habits and savings practices. We must take the economic climate recent retirees have faced into account. As a matter of principle, people do not deserve financial ruin. To suggest otherwise is too cruel for a faith-based discussion of economic justice.

While critically acclaimed films like *The Big Short* have highlighted how a select few made out with astronomic profits during the Great Recession, the more brutal truth behind the silver screen is that those financial windfalls came at the expense of ordinary people whose retirement accounts were absolutely decimated, or who did not have jobs that afforded them retirement benefits in the first place. In a span of months, workers who had contributed assiduously to their retirements saw decades of savings wiped out. Retirements were put on hold indefinitely, and many who had retired began to "unretire."

25. Erik Loomis, *A History of America in Ten Strikes* (The New Press, 2018), 5.

26. Jillian Harding, "More Older Americans Are 'Unretiring,'" *CBS News*, https://www.cbsnews.com/news/more-older-americans-are-unretiring/?ftag=COS-05-10aaa0g&utm_campaign=trueAnthem:+New+Content+, September 19, 2018, accessed September 20, 2018.

Fifty-three percent of boomers nearing retirement expect to postpone it, and 40 percent expect to work until they reach seventy,[27] and stories of retirees on fixed incomes who have had to choose between basic needs abound.

It would be easy—and entirely unhelpful—to try to proof-text scripture into positions against counting on one's retirement savings. Yes, Jesus preached in the Sermon on the Mount not to store up treasures for ourselves on earth. But a basic retirement income is not so much a treasure as a fundamental necessity. The overall arc of scripture compels us to care for orphans, widows, and those who are sick or disabled. Many of the elders in our lives inhabit multiple categories. Protecting their dignity is a biblical mandate, and churches are in a position to offer tangible and moral support.

A disproportionate number of our members, both lay and clergy, are older. The sheer size and dedication of its older constituency should mean that the church would be on the front lines in advocating for the financial security of retirees, and the ways in which congregations can do that are many.

Does your denomination operate a pension fund? Inquire about how they provide for the church's retirees and disabled persons, and what they need in order to do so most effectively. Ask about what they are doing to advocate for public policies to protect and assist those who are on their rolls, and how you can best assist them in that advocacy. If they are not engaged in such advocacy, ask what it would take to encourage them to do so. Ask them what resources they make available not just for clergy, but for laypeople, and if you see a hole in those resources, ask them to remedy it.

Is there a union local whose members are also members of your congregation? Ask them about how you can help the next time their union has to engage in peaceful protest or action on behalf of its retiring workers. Even after the decades of concerted union-busting, unions remain one of the organizations most focused upon the

---

27. Sarah O'Brien, "More Than Half of 60-Somethings Say They're Delaying Retirement," CNBC, https://www.cnbc.com/2018/04/27/delayed-retirement-is-in-the-cards-for-more-than-half-of-60-somethings.html, April 27, 2018, accessed September 20, 2018.

financial security of retirees. My doctoral research showed me that
union members sit next to us in the pews on Sundays and would welcome the church fostering conversations about important economic
issues that unions fight for every day, including financial security
during retirement, and how the church can faithfully engage those
issues.

Finally, there are often groups within our wider communities
that focus on retirees and their needs. What are their most immediate needs in advocating for the financial well-being of their members? How are they adapting to the new fiscal realities of seniors who
want—or need—to be able to retire but financially cannot afford to?
And can your community—spiritual or otherwise—foster empathy
and solidarity for retirees with the knowledge both that a basic livelihood is a human right and that most of us will be facing down retirement sooner or later for ourselves?

These suggestions are not exhaustive, but are intended to open up
possibilities to create change in your community, church, or denomination. Much like a gymnast leaping from a springboard, you can
try any number of things with the boost these suggestions hopefully
provide, and still land on your feet. It is my hope that you would
keep that metaphor in mind as younger generations emerge from high
school and college with new challenges their elders did not face, yet in
the face of those challenges are striving to do exactly what each generation has been told as they came of age: to land on their feet.

CHAPTER 7

Questions of Color
Slavery, Violent Removal, and
Reparations

*My wife, Carrie, her colleague Angele, Angele's husband, Thabiti, and I
slide into our seats in the cramped theater of the Interstate Firehouse
Cultural Center, a 1910s-era firehouse that sits in the heart of North
Portland, Oregon, and was repurposed as a community space by Portland's first black city commissioner.*

*We are there for a performance of Rich Rubin's play Left Hook, which
tells the story, inspired by historical events, of a black family that owned
and operated a boxing club in Portland's historic Albina neighborhood
in the 1970s. During that decade, numerous black-owned businesses
and homes were razed to make way for the Legacy Emanuel Medical
Center, where Carrie and Angele both work.*

*The all-black cast lays out just one of the dozens of scenarios of dis-
placement that played out across Albina during the 1970s, and have
played out across the United States for decades. After the performance,
we stay for a panel discussion with three older black residents of North
Portland, who dedicate over an hour of their time to offer their stories of
coming up in those days.*

*To take in both the play and the panel is to take in history in both
oral and written forms. Oral history is the history of the Bible as it was
handed down for generations before becoming the written manuscripts
we read. Oral history is also the history of the persecuted and the marginalized, the oppressed whose story is seldom told in museums and on
monuments, but has great value all the same.*

Upstairs from the theater is a small exhibit space. During a break, I venture up to look around, and I see some of the extensive documentation of the state of Oregon's black codes (or, anti-black codes). Oregon was established explicitly as an all-white state. Black settlers were banned under threat of floggings, and when Oregon was admitted as a state, its constitution contained a black exclusion clause.[1]

A small part of my mind harkens back to what I knew of the anti-Armenian codes passed along the West Coast in reaction to the influx of Armenian genocide refugees during and after the First World War. Municipalities banned Armenians from certain professions, or from settling in certain neighborhoods. The then-congressman of my current congressional district, the Washington Third, Albert Johnson, sponsored the 1924 Immigration Act that, among other things, virtually banned Armenian immigration to the United States for decades.

My home state of Kansas, which makes a big to-do about being a free state during the Civil War, also housed the state board that Linda Brown had to sue in the landmark Brown v. Board of Education. *I see that in any state, any region, the dominance of whiteness tempts us to disregard the deeply harmful aspects of our collective past that are inconvenient to the narratives we want to tell. In short, economic justice without racial justice is not full economic justice.*

As I rejoin my companions, I prepare to process the play's message with the reminder that the land I live and work on was not innocently obtained, and if I am to continue living and ministering here as an uninvited guest, I need to be living and ministering in a way that tells the truth about this land, and the inconvenient and violent past of those who took it—often in the name of the (primarily white) Christian interpretation of God.

To dismantle racism is to dismantle the primary justification for centuries of economic exploitation. "Racism is entirely about economics [and] labor. Always has been," anti-racism activist Bree Newsome

---

1. Cheryl A. Brooks, "Race, Politics, and Denial: Why Oregon Forgot to Ratify the Fourteenth Amendment," *Oregon Law Review,* vol. 83 (2004): 736–38.

Bass tweeted.[2] She sees racism and racial myths as justifications that the enslavement of—and ongoing discrimination against—black flesh vitally needed. To her, this history has "always been fundamentally about labor—not only labor—but (labor)'s the root of it."[3] Any toolkit for economic justice would be incomplete without tools for dismantling racism. And for the cause of faith-based, divinely inspired justice to be served, the majority-white church in the United States must take tangible and sacrificial actions—including financial reparations.

Living in the In-between: Benefiting from Whiteness Whilst Claiming Reparations

When I talk about reparations, I am speaking of efforts that require sacrificial financial expense on the part of primarily white communities for the benefit of primarily communities of color, and particularly black and indigenous communities in my geographic context of the United States. Reparations are necessary on a global scale as well, because of white oppression against primarily non-white peoples. One of the exceptions to that rule, however, concerns my Armenian ancestors and what they gave up to escape a genocide that killed the majority of the Armenian population in the Ottoman Empire.

On a basic theological level, I believe that the process of governments, universities, denominations, and individual congregations paying reparations urgently needs to accelerate. To fully live into the Gospel teachings on economic justice and racial/ethnic equity, there is no substitute for reparations. This I know from personal experience as the descendant of Armenian Genocide refugees who arrived in the United States in 1919 after fleeing their indigenous homelands in Anatolia.

My Armenian relatives did not just pick up and flee in a vacuum. They left behind not only the dead bodies of loved ones but also a

---

2. Bree Newsome Bass, https://twitter.com/BreeNewsome/status/1151479042270531586, July 17, 2019, accessed July 17, 2019.

3. Ibid., https://twitter.com/BreeNewsome/status/1151482494698569728, July 17, 2019, accessed July 17, 2019.

network of substantial personal and commercial resources from which they had made their livings for decades. Almost all of it was sacrificed, either abandoned by necessity or liquidated to enable their escapes into exile. Very little of it came with them in their journey across the vast expanse of Russia to Vladivostok, then from Yokohama, Japan, to the West Coast of the United States.

I had great-uncles, great-aunts, and a great-great-grandfather and great-great-grandmother who died during the genocide. That my great-grandparents survived was a combination of luck, resources, and timing. With the help of human smugglers in the Ottoman Empire and diaspora Armenians already settled in the United States, they were able to escape and slowly build for themselves a modest livelihood, but not like they had known in Anatolia. That life was irrevocably destroyed by the genocide.

Efforts at genocide recognition—which, as of this writing, the federal government of the United States has only just now embraced with resolutions being passed by both houses of Congress over President Donald Trump's objections[4]—are only the first part of the movement for genuine social and economic justice on behalf of the victims, survivors, and their descendants. The next part is the campaign for reparations, whose complexity makes the monumental, decades-long efforts at recognition look like a cakewalk by comparison. While I continue to believe federal recognition of the Armenian Genocide will happen in my lifetime, I have little expectation of any tangible direct restitution.

Why argue for reparations, then?

I used to be against the idea of reparations for genocide descendants and survivors. It seemed to be a form of blood money, the thought of which made me recoil. I wanted nothing to do with putting a monetary value on my family's pain, grief, and loss. As generation after generation of descendants in my family have been born, we have, on

---

4. Deirdre Shesgreen, "Senate Recognizes Armenian Genocide over Objections of Trump and Turkish Government," *USA Today*, https://www.usatoday.com/story/news/world/2019/12/12/senate-senate-recognizes-arrecognizes-armenian-genocide-over-objections-trump-and-turkish-government/4410046002/, December 12, 2019, accessed December 13, 2019.

balance, regained much of the financial security that was left behind over a century ago, due in no small part to the eventual inclusion of diaspora Armenians into whiteness, which only goes to show that whiteness is not a biological reality, but a social construct that expands and contracts to include and exclude who it needs to perpetuate itself.

While the material cost of the genocide was extremely high for my family—to say nothing of the human cost—I did not require reparations to live above the poverty line. I did not feel the personal urgency of requiring reparations to live in financial security, so demanding reparations was not my agenda.

During seminary, as I was immersed in the genuinely transformational teachings of professors committed to deepening our understanding of justice, I began to change my mind. I saw it would be the height of arrogance to say that ethnic Armenians worldwide required no reparations because I did not want them for myself. The older I got, the more compelling evidence that former Armenian holdings in Turkey continued to generate wealth for their current owners became. No truth-and-reconciliation commission, no blue-ribbon panel, no diplomatic process—however important, meaningful, or necessary—could take the place of the economic losses sustained by a people targeted for genocide.

Sometime during my first full-time pastorate in Longview, I came to the conviction that just as it would be arrogant for me to preemptively dismiss the need for reparations in the worldwide Armenian community, it would be unconscionably arrogant for me to argue for reparations for my own people and not for anybody else's. That flew in the face of everything that I believe the Gospel of Jesus Christ represents: genuine justice, tangible equity and equality, and salvation from both individual and systematic sinfulness.

Any discussion of reparations in the United States must, I strongly believe, include both black Americans due to centuries of chattel slavery, segregation, and Jim Crow, and also indigenous peoples for centuries of extermination and land theft. I have embraced a term that a former United States ambassador to Armenia, John Marshall Evans, used in his TED talk in Yerevan in 2011 to refer to this murderous history: "rolling genocide."[5] The displacement and extermination of indigenous tribes and cultures in the Americas is an ongoing sin rather than the single fell swoop other genocides sometimes are, and the fruits of that sin remain ongoing. To hear a genocide recognition advocate use the "rolling" to modify genocide gave me language to better comprehend and describe the dangerous fruits of a sin that has impacted me personally, as well as untold millions of others.

Because those fruits remain in the United States, tilting the scales in favor of whiteness, the responsibility for reparations falls on all white Americans, not only those whose ancestors owned slaves or fought for the Confederacy. As an ethnic Armenian, I benefit unduly from whiteness precisely because whiteness morphs to include us when it is in its best interests to do so. Those benefits must be tangibly counterweighted if economic and social equity is to ever be a realistic possibility.

For many Armenian Americans, including myself, whiteness expanded to include us in a variety of ways. The housing codes and oppressive immigration quotas of the 1920s fell by the wayside. In not all, but many, ways, we came to be seen as white, with all its attendant unearned privileges. Even though we live with a massive ethnicity-based trauma in our history, we Armenian Americans live in this in-between space where we sometimes feel the prejudice quite acutely, and we benefit from whiteness in a variety of situations.

Though my family came as refugees and never owned slaves, it is still incumbent upon me to contribute to reparations. Just because my ancestors were not slaveowners does not mean I do not benefit situationally from white privilege, or that the churches I have served have not benefited from being predominantly white churches. As an ordained pastor who is identified in census data as white, but as a result of his ethnicity has a legitimate claim to reparations himself, I can speak of both owing and being owed reparations. My hope is that my relatively uncommon circumstance can act as a way not of

5. John M. Evans, *Therefore, God Must Be Armenian* (Gomidas Institute, 2016), 73.

usurping the other narratives of peoples who are owed reparations, but to help explain the importance of reparations.

I am not writing as a substitute for the perspectives of black, Latinx, and indigenous peoples of the United States, or of the Americas more broadly. They, not I, are owed reparations from the United States as a direct result of the actions by local, state, and federal governments, non-governmental actors like churches and schools, and individual persons throughout United States history. My claim for reparations is directed at a different government, with different corporate and individual actors. My personal experience is not a substitute for, nor equivalent to, theirs, because whiteness eventually expanded to often—not universally, but often—include diaspora Armenians.

The perspectives of those who are owed reparations from the United States are not uniform. I cite several voices in this chapter, but I also strongly encourage you to seek them out and read them directly, invite them to speak at your events, and follow them on social media. Centering the perspectives of peoples of color in any discussion concerning reparations should be the order of the day. I have aimed to do so here.

The Doctrine of Discovery's Fruits of Destructiveness

One of the most critical aspects to remember about the case for reparations is that the history of economic oppression based on race was not limited to chattel slavery. Much as the oppression of American black people did not end with the abolition of chattel slavery, but continued in segregation, disenfranchisement, sharecropping, and more, so did the oppression of American indigenous tribes not end with their forced relocation to federally created reservations.

Fifty-seven years after passage of the Indian Removal Act that paved the way for the genocidal removals of indigenous tribes like the Trail of Tears, the 1887 Dawes Act was used to strip indigenous peoples of their reservation land under the guise of individualism. The Dawes Act granted indigenous individuals one hundred and sixty

acres of reservation land and the rest was repackaged for white colo-
nizers, which "undermined what was left of [indigenous] traditional
economies. [Indigenous persons] still labored . . . but within a racial
caste system that doomed them to endemic poverty, and which still
plagues the tribes today."[6]

The economic value of the forced labor by enslaved blacks from
1619 to 1865 is, by one estimate, $172 trillion in 2019 dollars[7]—
that is $172,000,000,000,000, to give a visual indication of how
many zeroes are involved. What is often flippantly dismissed as
ancient history by pundits and pastors alike who have benefited
from that history still impacts the present. The conversation, then,
is not about whether or not this history is ancient, but how best to
remedy its ongoing consequences.

Unfortunately, the history that gets taught of these actions and
their reverberating economic impacts is often fundamentally flawed.
It charitably presents the white explorers while erasing the indigenous
tribes and the wide-ranging impact that the arrival of the Europeans
had upon them. I would draw once more from John Marshall Evans
in the context of his "rolling genocide" term:

> We have a mixture of myths . . . How the good Englishmen—
> they usually don't talk about the other nationalities—the good
> Englishmen came to Virginia and met the Indians, of course
> some of the Indians came and attacked us, but we basically took
> their land. So, there is the myth, or story, we tell about winning
> the West. We don't talk about a 400-year rolling genocide.[8]

But we should. We must. And our talking about a four-hundred-
year rolling genocide ought to serve not as an end in and of itself,
but as a means to pave the way toward amends. A critical aspect of

---

6. Erik Loomis, *A History of America in Ten Strikes* (The New Press, 2018), 47–48.

7. Gillian Brockell, "Some White People Don't Want to Hear about Slavery at
Plantations Built by Slaves," *The Washington Post*, https://www.washingtonpost.com/
history/2019/08/08/some-white-people-dont-want-hear-about-slavery-plantations-built-by-
slaves/, August 8, 2019, accessed August 9, 2019.

8. John M. Evans, *Therefore, God Must Be Armenian* (Gomidas Institute, 2016), 72–73.

genocide is not just cultural erasure, but economic erasure—the taking and misappropriating of material resources and wealth, from land to jewelry to other valuables. Just as household goods were stripped from Jewish families during the Holocaust, so too were households and lands stripped from Armenians (including my own family) during the Armenian Genocide, and from black families via chattel slavery and indigenous families via this rolling genocide of which Evans speaks. Genocidal oppression, then, is fundamentally economic in nature as well as cultural and social. To speak of economic justice without also speaking of racial and ethnic justice, then, is an incomplete and inadequate conversation.

Against the crucible of such ghastly institutions and practices, the rise of liberation theology—the belief that God is on the side of the poor and explicitly endorses freeing them from systematic and economic oppression—in Latin America during the twentieth century should hardly be surprising. On the contrary, liberation theology serves as an explicit theological counterweight to centuries of colonialism's exploitative economic practices. Its development represents not a threat to Christian orthodoxy, but a continuation of it as expressed in scripture. A fundamental premise of liberation theology, drawn from Jesus's teachings in the Gospels, is that the last shall be first. This sentiment originates not in the post-Columbus Americas, but in the ancient Near East. While it may have been downplayed by white American Christianity, the church can purposefully choose to live it out, and in so doing find our own liberation. And one tangible way among many to begin living out the last being first is by putting reparations on the table.

Reparations can act as an integral component to a theological approach to liberation in the United States for the twenty-first century. Liberation from racism requires liberation from all aspects of it: the social inequities, the economic inequality, the erasure of culture, and more. For white people who have benefited from all of these over the course of time, sacrificially surrendering wealth is part of leveling the playing field, but also part of taking apart the status of whiteness as the default lens or experience in the United States, for with wealth often comes ability to control such narratives. To make the case for reparations from white American Christians on both the congregational/denominational level and the individual/personal level, we will use the remainder of this chapter to continue unpacking just some of the plethora of economic impacts of structural racism before making the case for financial reparations as one way to address at least some of those impacts.

Christianity, Chattel Slavery, and Wealth Inhibition in the Americas

Professor Thabiti Lewis, whom I introduced you to in the beginning of this chapter as one of the friends with whom my wife and I watched the play *Left Hook* in Portland, Oregon, shared in one of his books the story of his first-ever visit to the Negro Leagues Baseball Museum in my hometown of Kansas City, and how difficult the museum was for him to even locate:

> My struggle to locate the Negro Leagues Baseball Museum symbolizes the notion of race being an invisible relic of the past—its history difficult to locate. The Negro Leagues are a reminder that race is a construct. Just as the museum was difficult to locate, the form that race takes in the modern world can be difficult to articulate . . . but the museum's existence is evidence against denials of racism in America . . . Visiting [it] was a bittersweet experience because while it revealed the tenacity of the owners and players, it also reminded of America's harsh racial history as well as the one-sidedness of America's integration.[9]

I have my own memories of visiting the Negro Leagues Baseball Museum as a child growing up in Kansas City, but there is no way I could bring to bear a similar experience or perspective to such a visit, for the sole reason of how race has been used throughout US history to separate blackness from whiteness, and to make blackness less

---

9. Thabiti Lewis, *Ballers of the New School: Race and Sports in America* (Third World Press, 2010), 257–58.

visible or even invisible to whiteness. White Christianity has played an outsized role in this erasure, not only during the decades of chattel slavery, but in the post-slavery decades that followed, and this history of erasure has wrought substantial economic consequences.

Even long after emancipation of slaves was achieved, economic equity continues to face all manner of obstacles constructed by society and economy alike, and these obstacles were by no means unique to the Jim Crow South. During the 1950s and '60s, as the civil rights movement made monumental gains for civil rights, black persons residing in Chicago were cheated out of an estimated $3–4 billion in wealth through the practice of predatory housing contracts that disproportionately targeted black families who had little other means or legal recourse to obtain access to the real estate market.[10] That $3–4 billion figure comes from a span of just two decades in one US city, but it concerned predatory real estate climes that were present in, among other places, Portland, Oregon, and such predatory circumstances became the basis for the play *Left Hook.*

Nor have such exploitative housing practices ended. To cite but one contemporary example—one that intersects with the economic instability currently being experienced by American seniors that was detailed at the end of the previous chapter—black households are both disproportionately denied conventional mortgages in order to buy homes and targeted for foreclosure through predatory reverse mortgages that are marketed extensively to senior citizens. Of sixty-one cities reviewed in a 2018 study, forty-eight showed significantly higher rates of mortgage denials to black households compared to white households,[11] and even when adjusting for annual income levels, black households are six times more likely to face foreclosure over

---

10. Natalie Moore, "Contract Buying Robbed Black Families in Chicago of Billions," *WBEZ 91.5 Chicago,* https://www.wbez.org/shows/wbez-news/contract-buying-robbed-black-families-in-chicago-of-billions/d643ea19-2977-43d7-81c7-1d7a568c5c81?utm, May 30, 2019, accessed May 31, 2019.

11. Aaron Glantz and Emmanuel Martinez, "Kept Out," https://www.revealnews.org/article/for-people-of-color-banks-are-shutting-the-door-to-homeownership/, February 18, 2018, accessed June 13, 2019. It must be noted that such discrimination in lending practices is not limited to black households. The same study found discrimination in a number of metro areas against Latinx, Asian American/Pacific Islander, and/or indigenous households.

a reverse mortgage than white households.[12] The means of wealth and land theft from people and families of color may no longer be chattel slavery, but that does not mean that theft of wealth and land has ended in the United States.

Nor is the deleterious economic impact of centuries of racism limited to black American families. A couple different sections of this book have dealt specifically with the financial implications of access to healthcare, and American indigenous communities experience that challenge acutely. Kaitlin Curtice, a Christian author and member of the Potawatomi tribe, noted this reality in a column she wrote for the Christian publication *Sojourners* on the 2020 Democratic presidential primary debates: "On issues of health care, we must consider how little resources Native Americans are left with to care for their own mental, physical and even spiritual health . . . our well-being should be a part of every conversation for what it means to create a healthier America."[13] Disenfranchised from political and economic security for centuries as a direct result of American policy, indigenous peoples remain often unhelped by American policy.

The economic need for financial reparations, then, is an ongoing need, one that did not simply cease upon the end of the American Civil War in 1865. While chattel slavery may have ended in a strictly legal sense, it continued in an economic sense through the practices of sharecropping, land and property theft, segregation, voting disenfranchisement, and much more. And like the Negro Leagues Museum, the United States—and many of its predominant white churches— have chosen to make this history harder to access and read about. The exact opposite is required of us: a literacy of United States history fundamentally requires a literacy of its history of white supremacy, including the economic impacts of that history.

---

12. Nick Penzenstadler and Jeff Kelly Lowenstein, "Seniors Were Sold a Risk-Free Retirement with Reverse Mortgages. Now They Face Foreclosure," *USA Today,* https://www .usatoday.com/in-depth/news/investigations/2019/06/11/seniors-face-foreclosure-retirement-after-failed-reverse-mortgage/1329043001/, June 11, 2019, accessed June 13, 2019.

13. Kaitlin Curtice, "A Crucial Piece Missing in the Democratic Presidential Debates," *Sojourners,* https://sojo.net/articles/crucial-piece-missing-democratic-presidential-debates, June 28, 2019, accessed August 30, 2019.

White Christian Resistance to Civil Rights

My father, Gordon, whom you met all the way back in chapter 1, currently serves on the state of Kansas's Court of Appeals as one of its thirteen judges. He was born on May 17, 1954—the day the Supreme Court of the United States handed down its landmark 9–0 decision in *Brown v. Board of Education,* which laid the constitutional groundwork for the integration of the American school system. He says he may well have been fated to do this work of upholding the rights of others, first as an attorney and now as a judge. That the parent of a millennial was born the day that *Brown v. Board* was decided should also underscore just how little time has really passed since the dismantling of Jim Crow, especially relative to the decades of segregation and centuries of slavery that preceded it.

Those efforts to integrate and to dismantle segregation were only partially successful, however. White flight, school district gerrymandering, and an array of other tools were deployed in municipalities across the country to minimize the effects of newly mandated integration, and with those tools came the continued impoverishment of schools and school districts that predominantly serve black children, and children of color more broadly. The utilization of these tools had the dual—and, I would argue, intentional—effect of depriving poorer and majority-minority school districts of wealthier constituencies from which to draw financial and material resources. While these tools and their impacts were broad-based and hardly limited by regional geography, the history of white American Christianity is deeply interwoven with efforts to resist the integration of schools, and the advancement of civil rights and economic opportunities for non-whites more generally.

I touched on this in the final chapter of *Oregon Trail Theology,* but the American religious right as we understand it today did not come about, as is popularly thought to be the case, over the issue of abortion. Rather, as I explained in *OTT,* the coalescing of conservative, overwhelmingly white Christians into what we know today as the religious right was a backlash to the racial integration of schools and subsequent removal of tax-exempt status from private Christian "segregation academies." White evangelical opposition to abortion mostly came several years later. The fabric that binds and undergirds so much of white US Christianity is, and has historically been, racism. This toxic brew of Christianity and white racism represents a dangerous syncretism that has fueled so much of the public political witness of white Christianity to this day. Economic policies designed to aid impoverished families afford basic necessities are opposed on the grounds of mythical "welfare queens," an anti-black slur coined by Ronald Reagan as the Christian-led Moral Majority coalesced around him. Proposals to cut undocumented immigrants off from basic social services and welfare programs are rooted in the anti-brown xenophobia fostered by Donald Trump. And opposition to financial reparations coexists with the patently and easily disproven hypothesis that equality of opportunity somehow now exists in the United States.

But in the United States—and, indeed, across the worldwide church—the economic is also racial, and the racial is also economic. To speak of one is to speak of the other. And so in this book, we must. God's passion for justice demands nothing less of us.

Historical Revisionism and Holy Innocence

There is no escaping the statistical correlation between race and economic class in the United States. To the extent escape attempts have been made, they have been from the argument that there is causation, not merely correlation, in poverty as a direct result of race. Those efforts—typically from white people, often Christians— are patronizing at best and overtly racist at worst, with deprecating comments about the virtues of responsibility and addressing "black-on-black" crime (as though white people are doing a bang-up job of addressing "white-on-white" crime).

But the basic truth is that the fifty or so years of the post-civil rights movement era have hardly undone the economic damage wrought by a century-plus of Jim Crow, and three-plus centuries of chattel slavery. Indeed, that economic damage, instead of being halted or reversed, continues on in a number of devastating ways. And as long as there is a collective forgetfulness or apathetic shrug at the history of American economic prosperity being built on the backs of non-white peoples, I believe that this pattern will continue.

To resist this pattern of forgetfulness, it is imperative to remember that at its core, chattel slavery was a dehumanizing, moneymaking enterprise built on the fundamental premise of white supremacy over non-white peoples. No talk of "states' rights," no absolution of individual slaveowners, no moral obfuscation can ever be permitted to erase that basic historical reality.

Yet permit it the United States has—or, at least, we have permitted time and again attempts to erase that reality. From our history textbooks to our politicians' speeches to even some of our own pastors' sermons, the trappings of historical revisionism loom large in our public—and theological—discourse. The historicity and consequences of racism may seldom get addressed in a majority-white church outside of perhaps some lip service on Martin Luther King Jr. Sunday, and even when they are addressed, it is as much with an aim to absolve our theological and national forebearers by way of mitigating factors, lukewarm justifications, and outright excuses.

This revisionism often takes the form of arguments meant to lessen, soften, or even blur altogether the deleterious effects of the United States' historical sins of chattel slavery, the slave trade, and the rolling genocide of indigenous peoples. By simultaneously insisting that racism exists only on an individual—rather than also a systemic or systematic—level, and then absolving racist individuals of both history and the present, the reality of racism is swept under the proverbial rug, not to be addressed lest it be branded as "divisive" by those who have a vested interest in keeping racism hidden beneath that proverbial rug. By so rarely seriously grappling with the United States' history of racism, American political and theological leaders alike make it easier for this history to be mistreated and mishandled. Without an understanding of how we as a people got here, white American Christianity is apt to see racism and bigotry in an abstract vacuum rather than being informed by hundreds of years of history, including church history.

It is an error of titanic proportions to approach racism in such a vacuum, as though it exists only in the hearts of individuals and not in the trappings of contemporary civilization. Yet it remains a mistake that, anecdotally, I see made frequently—potentially on purpose—by a great many Christian churches, pastors, and leaders.

I say "on purpose" because by now, with what we know about American history and American Christian history in particular, attempts to shield that history from critical scrutiny are not innocuous or innocent. The holy innocence of whiteness is something that must be urgently cast aside if American Christianity is to ever truly address the breadth and depth of how it has contributed to racism across both history and geography. Historical revisionism is a frequently used tool in the service of the holy innocence of whiteness, but is by no means the only such manifestation of this mindset.

To adhere to the holy innocence of whiteness is to place in a position of implicit guilt the Messiah and namesake of Christianity, who almost surely was not the fair-skinned blond or light-brown-haired man Americans usually see him depicted as. To adhere to the holy innocence of whiteness is to place in a position of implicit guilt all those who in outward appearance may resemble that selfsame Messiah, or who are even darker in color. And to adhere to the holy innocence of whiteness is to cast aside what is known to be true about how this implicit guilt on the basis of skin color has been so interwoven into the fabric of American culture, governance, and religion. Instead of indulging its own white guilt, the predominantly white American church must be aware of how it has attempted to pass off legal and moral guilt onto its siblings and neighbors of color. Even the unraveling of even some of that fabric since the civil rights movement has still left intact much of its toxic tapestry.

That tapestry includes the economic statistics laid out in the beginning of this section. The wealth gap between white and non-white Americans (and especially black, Latinx, and indigenous Americans) remains real and likely far deeper than many white Americans understand. That wealth gap exists as a direct result of centuries of chattel slavery, land theft, and extermination in the name of white American exceptionalism. And it continues to be fueled by policies that are meant to inhibit any progress toward economic equity. This is not only a problem stemming from past sins like chattel slavery. It is a problem stemming from present sins as well.

To do more than simply offer Band-Aids or stopgaps, more radical steps like financial reparations must be put on the table. And crucially, doing so must be understood not as yet another act of white *noblesse oblige* or patronizing beneficence, but rather as an act of justice and the paying of a massive outstanding moral and economic debt. Charity and justice are not identical, and Christianity should have a role to play in highlighting the differences between the two. And any conversation about reparations must be aware of those important differences.

Putting Reparations on the Table

So how do these conversations even begin in the still largely racially homogenous spaces of white American Christianity? There may not be a true apples-to-apples precedent, but there are several possible templates that come to mind, each from different contexts that the church can look to for guidance and inspiration in considering its own moral imperative concerning reparations.

Reparations are, as an American government policy, not unprecedented, even if the times when reparations were made were likely inadequate, and certainly belated. During the civil rights movement of the 1950s and '60s, Japanese Americans also called for reparations to the Japanese Americans who were interned in camps by the federal government during the Second World War. It took twenty-plus years of organizing, campaigning, and lobbying, but in 1988, the federal government approved reparations of $20,000 (approximately $44,000 in 2020 dollars) for every living Japanese American internment camp survivor. Additional funds for reparation payments, accompanied by a formal apology from then-president George H.W. Bush, were approved by the federal government in 1992.

That $20,000, paid out over forty years after the fact, represents a relative pittance for three-plus years of racist and unjust incarceration should be self-evident, and that is before the economic costs of internment to the Japanese American community are taken into account. While earning my doctorate at Seattle University, I saw first-hand some of the lingering economic consequences of internment in Seattle's Japanese American community. Businesses, homes, and properties had to be abandoned. Livelihoods and sources of income were shut off. And in basic, even mundane, everyday terms, nobody wants a three-year gap on their resume.

The formal-apology-coupled-with-individual-cash-payments offers one template for reparations, although it does leave some glaring gaps. One is that cash does not by itself return stolen land—a point that the Sioux nation has been making for decades in their steadfast refusal to accept financial damages for their ancestral lands confiscated by the federal government.[14] Another is ensuring that the culture of the people targeted for slavery, genocide, or internment is not erased. Money by itself does not ensure the preservation of culture; rather, money must be explicitly purposed for preventing the erasure of cultures. Institutions like the Wing Luke Museum in Seattle dedicate themselves to such preservation efforts (in Wing Luke's case, of the Japanese American narrative), but they often must rely heavily on private donations. Reparative funds could help offset the reliance on private donors.

Universities and denominations that benefited financially from chattel slavery could elect to do what Georgetown University did, in making light of their past slaving practices and directing reparative efforts toward any known descendants of the persons enslaved by their denomination. Georgetown offering known descendants the

---

14. The Sioux nation's claim to South Dakota's Black Hills made it all the way to the Supreme Court of the United States in the case *United States v. Sioux Nation of Indians* (1980), where the entire Supreme Court, save for one dissenting justice, ruled that the Sioux nation had never received financial redress for the lands forcibly taken from them. The Sioux nation has refused financial compensation on the grounds that doing so would recognize the legitimacy of the confiscation of their ancestral lands. In instances like this, the church must be keenly aware that financial recompense of an outstanding debt may not be the reparative solution, even though it may be in other instances.

same preferential status as legacy applicants is a very small step—and a problematic one, as legacy admissions tend to overwhelmingly benefit white and wealthier applicants. Believing more was required for the sake of social justice, the Georgetown student body voted overwhelmingly in the spring of 2019 to enact a $27.20-per-semester student fee (symbolic of the 272 slaves the university once sold) to go toward financial reparations.[15]

Schools such as Cambridge University in England are presently studying and reckoning with precisely how they benefited from colonialism and chattel slavery, but the studies by themselves are surely inadequate if not followed up by genuine efforts at education, self-reflection, and reparation. Georgetown's efforts are by no means perfect or even adequate, but as more ideas emerge for reparation that extract a financial cost from the institutions and peoples who benefited the most from past economic exploitation, the church cannot afford to simply ignore them or pretend that these ideas are being offered. Divinity schools such as Virginia Theological Seminary and Princeton Theological Seminary now constitute a vanguard of schools that have taken the step of setting aside millions of dollars for reparation funds as public acts of atonement for benefiting from slavery.[16] These actions have sprung forth from a context of increased public dialogue over the topic of reparations, spurred primarily by black and indigenous voices. As in the scriptures, prophetic voices informed by our past are speaking to us, and we should listen.

The listening and active responding of white Christianity can—and should—take place on the individual level as well. Just as there are ways for institutions like churches and universities to make reparative efforts, so too are there ways for individuals to do so. One example from my local area is that of Portland-based anti-racism and LGBTQ

---

15. Susan Surluga, "Georgetown Students Vote in Favor of Reparations for Enslaved People," *Washington Post*, http://www.washingtonpost.com/education/2019/04/12/georgetown-students-vote-favor-reparations-slaves, April 12, 2019, accessed January 31, 2020.

16. Tom Gjelten, "With Plans to Pay Slavery Reparations, Two Seminaries Prompt a Broader Debate," National Public Radio, October 29, 2019, https://www.npr.org/2019/10/29/774217625/with-plans-to-pay-slavery-reparations-two-seminaries-prompt-a-broader-debate, accessed December 13, 2019.

activist Tori Williams Douglass. Douglass has spent years organizing a variety of anti-racism efforts on social media, drawing in part on her past as a practicing Christian who came to realize that the nature of the Christianity she was raised with enabled oppression even with its choice of words and language. As she says, "It took me a very long time to gain the language necessary to articulate how immoral and unethical it is to strip someone of their dignity and autonomy, because that was not language we ever used in the church."[17]

Douglass set out to change that language—inside and outside the church. For years, she has organized a series of campaigns on social media designed to change the way race and sexuality are understood, including in terms of their financial implications. One such campaign is the weekly #ReparationsFriday campaign, which began as #Fund-BlackWomenFriday and, according to Douglass, has raised over $20,000 in individual donations to black and indigenous women. The driving idea behind #ReparationsFriday/#FundBlackWomen-Friday is that because black people—and black women in particular—do so much unpaid emotional labor living in a predominantly white country and educating the white people in their lives, and that this labor should be paid for, with additional donations distributed to black women in circumstances of financial need. Douglass engages this campaign on Fridays, when many employees are typically paid, and purposefully frames it as extending this payday for peoples' labor that had previously gone unpaid and, often, unappreciated. She uses common cash transfer apps like Venmo and Cash App to facilitate the transfer of wealth from donors to black women, promotes that work on social media, and encourages black women to share their own screen names for those apps to facilitate donations to them directly.

Tori Williams Douglass emphasizes in her own writing and teaching that until society—through the government—collectively engages in a process of reparations, the offering of reparations is an individual responsibility, and that those of us who benefit from whiteness must

---

17. Andrew Jankowski, "Profiles in Queer Excellence and Resilience," *Portland Mercury*, https://www.portlandmercury.com/queer-issue-2019/2019/06/06/26594518/profiles-in-queer-excellence-and-resilience, June 6, 2019, accessed June 13, 2019.

practice it.[18] On an individual level, the transfer of wealth from white households to black households via campaigns like #Reparations-Friday can act as an explicit recognition of the labor and presence of black people that, as Lewis notes in the excerpt that I quoted earlier in this passage, historically has gone unseen or erased. It also claims autonomy and proactive change by not simply waiting for reparations to take place on a communal or governmental level. That can—and should—be advocated and agitated for, but in the interim, the individual practice of reparations still matters.

I would argue that this is a crucial theological component of reparation—that the visibility of others, whom Christianity holds as being made in the image of God in Genesis 1 but who have been erased by historically white interpretations of Christianity, is honored. Transfer of wealth is the practical aspect of reparations, but that practicality needs to be accompanied by a conscious—and, in Christian terms, theological—shift in our understanding of race and racism to take apart the mindsets that make whiteness the default and replace them with mindsets that center non-whiteness.

Being born and raised a diaspora Armenian and citizen of the United States means that I have simultaneously seen my whiteness centered as the default or ideal, and seen my ethnicity highlighted as something vaguely or safely exotic. Undoing that social programming is an ongoing process that I undertake every day, and will continue undertaking for the rest of my life. Along the way, I have realized that being a diaspora Armenian means that the connection to my own ancestors' homeland was taken away from me by way of genocide when the only options available to my ancestors were exile or near-certain death. That is part of genocide's destructiveness, and part of our loss, for with the loss of life comes the loss of culture. The continual upholding and centering of whiteness—both before and after the abolition of chattel slavery—must be included in this assessment. And while there perhaps can be no price affixed to that loss in terms of dollars and cents, there can be amounts proffered as reparations to

18. Tori Williams Douglass, "How to be a Good White Friend," https://www.toriglass.com/my-writing/2019/6/30/how-to-be-a-better-white-friend, July 1, 2019, accessed July 2, 2019.

ensure the preservation of a culture that was targeted for extinguish-
ment. There can also be amounts dedicated toward leveling the economic playing field that was purposefully laid in a lopsided manner
from the moment Christopher Columbus set foot on Hispaniola in
1492.

And what of purposefully theological approaches toward reparations? Jemar Tisby makes the compelling argument in his 2019 book,
The Color of Compromise, to approach reparations like the Year of
Jubilee of Leviticus. He suggests that churches "could pool resources
to fund a massive debt forgiveness plan for black families. Or they
could invest large amounts into trust funds for black youth. . . . These
monies could fund educational opportunities or down payments on
houses. . . . Churches could also invest money in local public schools
that predominately serve black students."[19]

The diversity of Tisby's suggestions should make plain that there
is no one-size-fits-all program, and that primarily white religious
institutions interested in making amends would do well to carefully
examine what needs exist where they are located, and then reach out
to address those needs in partnership with communities of color in
their area. Resources for discernment regarding matters where the
spiritual intersects with the financial already abound for churches and
denominations, and to harness them as part of a broader conversation
surrounding reparations is an important next step for predominantly
white Christian communities to take.

I would even go so far as to say this: a predominantly white congregation that is large and/or wealthy enough to successfully plan and
execute a capital campaign should, as a matter of theological conscience, incorporate a reparative aspect into their capital campaign
and fund it before any of the other priorities the campaign is striving
to pay for. Without such an effort, I would consider any such capital
campaign—or any selling or buying of real property—by a congregation to be fundamentally incomplete from a theological perspective.

---

19. Jemar Tisby, *The Color of Compromise* (Zondervan, 2019), 200.

These spiritual and financial efforts may well pinch congregations and denominations that are already trying desperately in an era of slashed budgets and staffs to avoid a mentality of scarcity. But we frankly should feel that pinch. To borrow from C.S. Lewis in *Mere Christianity,* there should be things we want to do but cannot do because our giving precludes us from doing so. In this particular case, I would substitute "reparations" for "giving." There should be things the white church and historically primarily white universities cannot afford because our reparative expenditures prevent us from affording them.

Feeling pinched by financial efforts to mitigate a historic sin should likewise be understood theologically. It inflicts discomfort, like the donning of a sackcloth or a hair shirt, and that was partly the point of such public displays of mourning and repentance in ancient Israel. Repentance, like grace, cannot come cheaply. It is far too important to be had at bargain basement prices. And I know from personal experience that the labors of reparation and repentance are ongoing. I myself remain very much a work in progress, and my words here are a reflection of that continuous process. What I offer here are not so much conclusions meant to close off discussion, but rather springboards for discerning potential ways forward. Discernment is a spiritual gift of Christianity, but one that the church can sometimes do a better job of teaching and fostering in its people. And the cause of racial and economic justice cries out for the deepest, most serious discernment and listening from American Christians whose churches and denominations have historically benefited from racism, and who now have the epochal opportunity to make at least some semblance of tangible amends.

Epilogue

Rest on the Seventh Day

On the sixth day God completed all the work that he had done, and on the seventh day God rested from all the work that he had done. God blessed the seventh day and made it holy, because on it God rested from all the work of creation.

Genesis 2:2–3

Creation is work.

Creation is not simply a thing, or a state of being. Creation is a verb, a state of doing, crafting, and laboring.

Creation is work.

All the work of creation, Genesis says, caused God to rest. And because God rested, that day became blessed and holy in God's sight.

We have emerged together from seven chapters on mighty, soul-sized topics concerning peoples' livelihoods in the face of Christian social teaching, and the modern world's disregard for those livelihoods and that teaching in its pursuit of making the wealthy even wealthier.

That is a lot to have to work through and process together. It is okay to give yourself some time to let these topics simmer. Tend to yourself if you are feeling overwhelmed by the enormity of what God calls us to accomplish.

Yes, much of what I shared here, especially in the first chapter and last two chapters, is of urgent import for people living today, but just as Rome was not built in a day, neither will the kingdom of heaven be built here on earth in a day—at least, not by human hands alone.

It is important to give our weary and scarred hands a rest so that they may continue to do the work of picking us back up, reaching out in love for others, and remaking a world for the rich into a world that is rich for all.

We have our "big picture" goal of a world that provides for the poor, the oppressed, and the marginalized. Truthfully, we have always had that goal. We may have forgotten about it, but it has always been present. Within our greater, soul-sized goals, we also have smaller, day- and week-sized goals. One of those daily goals, the Bible tells us, is bread—sustenance and survival. One of those weekly goals the Bible similarly tells us is rest and rejuvenation. Even in the direst of circumstances, those daily and weekly goals must remain.

In the preface to his 2014 book *Sabbath as Resistance*, Walter Brueggemann points out the importance of the commandment of keeping the Sabbath day holy, even during Israel's time in the wilderness: "Even in such a marginal context, with daily need for bread that is given for the day, provision is made for the Sabbath. Israel cannot store up bread for more than one day; except . . . on the sixth day Israel may store up enough for the seventh day so that it can rest on that day."[1]

However marginal—or marginalized—you may feel, please do not neglect your own importance to God. Do not set aside the need that God has recognized for you to rest. For if God, the maker of heaven and earth and all that is seen and unseen required rest, then it is far too much to ask of ourselves to not require any rest. The Protestant-capitalist work ethic may not make such allowances, so we must.

May your rest become a part of your resistance to being marginalized. Allow yourself to be worthy of the rest you take. Do not feel like you have to justify your time off, and do not let yourself feel that you must make up for the time you do take off. The time we take to rest serves a holy, divine purpose. Let that purpose be enough, as it was enough for God.

Purposefulness should not be limited to our labor. Our understanding of it must be expanded to include our rest from our labors as well. Only when recovery from our labors is placed on the same level of importance to our wellbeing as our labor itself can we move forward with the healthier understanding of work, dignity, and basic economic justice.

---

1. Walter Brueggemann, *Sabbath as Resistance: Saying No to the Culture of Now* (Westminster John Knox Press, 2014), xiii.

For God, such purposefulness was never in doubt. Genesis says nothing about God needing to justify the day of rest to Godself; indeed, God appears more concerned with justifying the day of rest for us, perhaps because God recognizes that we may well fail to understand its importance to our lives. As is so often the case, what appears to be supremely evident to God remains a controversial question to us.

I hope that this book will serve as a tool to navigate these ongoing controversial questions of workers' rights, labor, and Christian teaching. As the obfuscation of what is in the best interest of the poor and working peoples continues by those who have a vested interest in ensuring that only crumbs remain for the least among us, we desperately need moral compasses and spiritual GPS devices to cut through that spiritual misdirection as much as ever.

Coping with such misdirection can be a spiritually exhausting experience in and of itself, and only adds to our need for rest and renewal in an era where real news is labeled as fake news, and where previous avatars for objective truth now proclaim that there was really no such thing all along. If living in this world for the past four-plus years has mentally and emotionally fatigued you, it is not just you. The fatigue is real.

I know because I have felt that fatigue myself—and still feel it, even as I try to recover. I am writing these words to you as I try to set my own fatigue aside for a few brief moments during a couple of days of vacation that Carrie and I have planned along with our daughter, Sadie, that coincide with a retreat in western Montana where I am speaking. We purposefully set aside the additional time to be family, to see old friends, and to rest and relax together. While guest speaking represents labor for me, I hope that others can find rest and renewal as well as inspiration. Part of retreating is to take not just geographical leave but emotional leave from our labors. It is the blessing of spiritual vacation from labor.

Knowing all of that, I confess that it still often feels selfish, even decadent, for me to take time for vacation. That is the time-honored Protestant-capitalist work ethic in me, honed over years of having to set boundaries with my work, and after being raised by a pair of workaholic parents. It is part of my lifelong experience of American Christian culture; I know it is unhealthy in many ways, and counter-programming it is an ongoing challenge for me. Perhaps such counter-programming presents a challenge for you as well. The unhealthiness of our collective obsession with overwork is something that communicates that rest is somehow sinful or must be justified, rather than simply being something one does to preserve their physical, mental, and spiritual well-being. To transgress that ethic and culture can very easily feel sinful, even when we may intellectually know that it is not.

Taking that rest, then, is countercultural in the purest sense of the term.

It is also biblical. Divine. Holy and sacred.

If hearing those words gives you permission to rest in anticipation of the labors that lie ahead, then we have ended this particular written journey together at a healthier destination.

Writing this much has been a labor of mind, soul, and heart for me. The words came in fits and starts, sometimes cascading over me like a waterfall, and sometimes drying up into a desert as forbidding as the Sahara. I would not have wanted these words to be born any other way. But it was most certainly *work*.

If reading my words has felt similarly spiritually laborious—hopefully not because my words did not resonate with you, but because they spoke to a reality you knew in your bones to be true—then I invite you to take a Sabbath rest alongside me. We each can, and should, rest from the work this book demands of us.

In that period of rest, my prayer is that we will both find what we have been searching for—what humanity has spent millennia searching for—but what we have not found nearly often enough: a source of life in a world that peddles largely in death.

The God who authored our lives likewise authored that sort of life-giving rest.

Take it. Relish it. Find resurrection and renewal in it.

Then, once we have rested, let us begin our divinely inspired labors again. Together.

Missoula, Montana
August 2019

ACKNOWLEDGMENTS

On Earth as It Is in Heaven is my second book, and I hope it has not fallen into the writerly trap expressed in the children's rhyme "second verse, same as the first, a little bit louder and a little bit worse." If *On Earth as It Is in Heaven* does evade that trap, it is only because of the guidance that I received along the way from my fellow travelers. My gratitude overflows for the following:

My editor at Church Publishing, Milton Brasher-Cunningham. Thank you for believing in me and my writing not once, but twice in our time thus far of working together. Knowing that you make me a better writer is the trust every author hopes to have in their editor.

My thesis committee at Seattle University's School of Theology and Ministry—Rev. Dr. Michael Reid Trice (chair), Dr. Sharon Henderson Callahan, and Rev. Dr. Richard Cunningham. As I noted in the preface, this book was inspired by my work at SU-STM, and I am grateful for the oversight and guidance you provided me and my work each step of the way on that journey. In addition to Seattle University, I continue to remain thankful for my other alma maters, Lewis & Clark College in Portland, Oregon, and the Pacific School of Religion in Berkeley, California, for the instruction and community in being first a student, and now an alum, at those schools.

The people of First Presbyterian Church of Vancouver, Washington, and their lead pastor, my friend and colleague Rev. Dr. Josh Rowley, whom I served as their interim director of family ministries while writing and editing *On Earth as It Is in Heaven*. Thank you for supporting this writing part of my call to ministry with your flexibility and grace. I likewise remain forever grateful to the previous parishes I have served—First Christian Church (Disciples of Christ) of Longview, Washington, as their senior pastor, and First Christian Church (Disciples of Christ) of Concord, California, and their then-senior pastor, Rev. Dr. Russ Peterman (currently of University Christian Church in Fort Worth, Texas), as one of their student associate ministers.

My ecclesiastical superior, Rev. Sandy Messick, for supporting this minister through the unexpected twists and turns of his vocational journey as an ordained Disciples of Christ pastor.

My webmaster and friend, Chris Trejbal, and his wife, Peggy. I am grateful most importantly for your friendship, but also for your care in helping me create and maintain an online home for myself and my writing that is true to who I am and what I want my ministry to be.

My community of friends and *Oregon Trail Theology* readers on social media. I do this work for you, and I hope my *koinonia* love for you shines through in my words on the page.

Finally, writing for a living can be a mightily isolating and vulnerable existence, and my family is one of the biggest reasons I am able to cultivate the spiritual energy for the vocation of writing. Additionally, I had just begun writing *On Earth as It Is in Heaven* in earnest when I became a father for the first time, and my family was the solid rock to which I clung as I navigated the newfound waters of parenthood. My in-laws, Bill and Nancy Hamby, in addition to being stalwart sources of spiritual encouragement, are wonderful grandparents-slash-babysitters. My parents, Gordon Atcheson and Cheryl Pilate, and my sister, Katherine Atcheson, have been beyond generous in their support, both in the form of many cross-country visits and in the form of gifts of toys, clothes, books, and anything else we could have possibly needed. And my wife, Carrie Atcheson, is both a loving life partner and a devoted mother to our daughter, Sadie. My days and years with you are what define goodness in my life, my love.

DISCUSSION QUESTIONS

Chapter 1

1. What are some of the beliefs you hold about the causes of poverty and inequality? How do you think you have come by those beliefs?

2. What do you remember being taught about poverty when you were younger, whether by a parent, a pastor, a teacher, a coach, etc.? Has what you were told proven to be true over time or not?

3. What is your impression of how the church addresses poverty in its message and mission? In what ways do you see the church faithfully addressing poverty? In what ways do you see the church falling short?

4. Eric covers several symptoms of economic injustice in this chapter, such as education inequality, housing prices and homelessness, food deserts, and healthcare costs. Do you see one or more of these symptoms affecting your current community? If so, what are churches in your area doing to meet that need, or what could they do differently?

5. In what ways do you see those symptoms interacting with one another (for instance, how might a lack of access to wholesome foods affect the healthcare a person receives)? Are there any that you see as particularly interconnected, and if so, why?

Chapter 2

1. How is the Tanakh taught in your religious community (if you belong to one)? Is it framed in its own terms or mostly in relation to, say, the New Testament or subsequent church teachings?

2. *Were any of the Tanakh passages utilized in this chapter already well known to you? Were any of them a surprise? On what basis do you tend to attach importance to a particular passage of scripture?*

3. *Eric uses the corvee as an example from ancient history of the timeless phenomenon of the exploitation of the labor of the poor. What are some ways in which the corvee continues to exist today but in a different form and under a different name? What actions can you take in fighting against their use?*

4. *What relationship do you see the Tanakh prophets having with the kings of their respective nations? What relationship do you see present-day prophets having with the presidents and rulers of modern nations?*

5. *How do you differentiate between wrath or anger, and a passion for justice? How have you seen the latter get mistaken for the former in the church, or in the world more broadly?*

Chapter 3

1. *How does your impression of the New Testament compare or contrast to your impression of the Tanakh? Where might those similarities or differences in impression have come from in your life, and how do they comport with what is actually in the texts?*

2. *What is the relationship that you see between the spiritual and material dimensions of the church's mission as taught throughout the New Testament? How does each dimension impact or feed the other?*

3. *Eric talks in this chapter about fostering a hermeneutic of totality—of interpreting the Bible on the basis of how extensively it covers certain topics compared to other topics. What topics do you see most frequently brought up at church, and do they correspond with what the Bible seems to most frequently address? If not, why do you think that might be?*

4. How do portrayals of Jesus and Mary in popular culture (such as in movies and artwork) accurately or inaccurately reflect what each of them teaches us about wealth and justice? In what ways might we have made Jesus in our image and not the other way around?

5. What has your relationship with, or impression of, religious apocalypticism been like? How might apocalyptic texts in the Bible serve as "good news" for the poor, even if those texts sometimes are misused today?

Chapter 4

1. Are there particular events or eras in religious history that stand out to you as particularly important or formative—whether to you personally or to the world? Why do those events or eras stand out to you?

2. In what ways do you see feudal hierarchies like the lord-peasant or patron-creator relationships continued in today's economic systems? What do you imagine the writers of the scriptures might have to say about those relationships?

3. Eric uses atonement theory as an example of how the economics of a particular era shaped the theology taught in the church for almost a millennium. What have you been taught, or what do you believe, that may have been influenced by the economics of a past era?

4. How have you seen the economic practice of speculation impact the financial security of communities, churches, and individuals—including potentially yourself or your own communities? Have those impacts been positive or negative?

5. In what ways do you see wealth—and the generation of wealth—worshiped in popular culture? Who do you see being helped the most by such wealth-worship? Who do you see being harmed the most?

Chapter 5

1. *What do you remember being originally taught about the origins of the United States? What cultural, economic, or religious influences may have impacted what you were originally taught? Do you still see what you were originally taught as accurate, or mostly accurate?*

2. *If you belong to a religious community, what official teachings (if any) are you aware of that it has made concerning economic justice and/or labor rights? What scriptures, history, and/or theology has informed those teachings? If your church and/or denomination has not offered any such teachings, why might that be the case?*

3. *In this chapter, Eric shares some of his findings from his research into Christian values and labor organizing in his local context. What, if anything, of what he found resonates with you in your context? What surprises you? What further questions do his findings raise for you?*

4. *Have you ever participated in some sort of labor organizing (forming a union, striking, etc.)? What are your own recollections of the experience? If you have not, what has been your impression of any of the organized labor actions you have witnessed or seen in the news?*

5. *What possibilities do you see for religious involvement on behalf of workers, or on behalf of economic justice more broadly? What obstacles might need to be overcome, and what resources might be needed?*

Chapter 6

1. *If you are a millennial, what are some of the economic challenges you feel your generation faces more acutely than other generations? If you are not a millennial, how do you see millennials and their economic obstacles framed in the news you consume and the social media platforms you frequent?*

2. *If you are not a millennial, what is an economic obstacle you recall having to face in the past, or are worried about facing in the future? If you are a millennial, do you have faith that your economic concerns or obstacles will ever be alleviated in the future, and why or why not?*

3. *Eric discusses how gendered economic concerns such as access to contraception and paid family leave are inherently justice issues. Nevertheless, many congregations and denominations have opposed such access. Why do you think that is, and what can or should be done to change that?*

4. *Eric also highlights how older generations such as the baby boomers are being adversely affected by the growing inequality of wealth. How have you seen the relationship with wealth change from generation to generation, for either good or bad? How might the needs of each generation affect their relationship with wealth?*

5. *What are some ways in which an intergenerational congregation might be uniquely positioned to address topics of poverty? In congregations that are made up mostly of one or two generations, how might intergenerational dialogue on poverty be fostered?*

Chapter 7

1. *What do you remember being taught about US history concerning racist acts of oppression like chattel slavery, Jim Crow, the displacement of indigenous tribes, the internment of Japanese Americans, etc.? What does the memory of those institutions evoke for you today?*

2. *How do you see historical revisionism used in conversations— whether in your own life or in the public sphere—about the above subjects, or in conversations about similar topics like genocide or the slave trade? How does historical revisionism*

impact our theologies and understandings of what it means to be church (or any other religious community)?

3. *In what ways does racism affect day-to-day life in your local community or context? How might your answer to that question be informed by your ethnicity, race, or skin color?*

4. *More specifically, what are some of the economic implications of race and ethnicity both globally and locally? How have those implications been informed by US and world history?*

5. *What could tangible economic reparations look like in your local community or context? What about in your religious community or context?*